KU-204-563

▲ Windsurfing along Maui's shores

and east − windward − coasts, which are characterized by steep sea cliffs, inaccessible stream-cut valleys, and dense tropical vegetation, and has a drier and less fertile aspect on the west and south − leeward − sides. Additionally, the two distinct volcanoes each have their own wet and dry sides.

Like its neighbors, Maui has concentrated almost all of its tourist development on its sunbaked leeward shorelines, with its major resorts either lying north of

▼ Fruit stand, East Maui

▼ Taking a boat tour

historic Lahaina in West Maui, like Kāʻanapali and Kapalua, or along the southwestern flanks of Haleakalā in what's known as South Maui, like Kīhei, Wailua, and Mākena. These resorts offer safe sandy beaches, ideal conditions for watersports, and all the amenities the modern vacationer could ask for. That said, should you tire of endlessly meandering between brunch and beach, there's plenty to see and do elsewhere on the island – from strolling the streets of old Lahaina and biking down from the summit of Haleakalā to hiking alongside waterfalls at ʻOheʻo Gulch and shopping for Hawaiian music.

▲ Sunset over Molokini

DIRECTIONS

WRITTEN AND RESEARCHED BY

Greg Ward

ROUGH
GUIDES

NEW YORK • LONDON • DELHI

www.roughguides.com

Contents

Introduction to

Maui

Thanks to its superb beaches, ravishing tropical scenery, an exhilarating range of activities, and magnificent hotels, the island of Maui can justly claim to be the world's most

▲ Green sea turtle

glamorous destination. The slogan Maui No Ka 'Oi – "Maui Is the Best" – may gloss over the fact that it's both the second largest and the second youngest of the Hawaiian chain, and ranks a distant second to Oahu in terms of annual visitors, but for island inhabitants and devotees alike the "Valley Isle" has a cachet its neighbors could never match.

Maui is what's known as a "volcanic doublet," consisting of two originally separate but now overlapping volcanoes. The older of the two, known to geologists as Mauna Kahalawai, has eroded to become a serrated ridge that's usually referred to as the West Maui Mountains; it's now dwarfed by the younger Haleakalā to the southeast. Around four hundred thousand years ago, Haleakalā dominated the landmass known as "Maui Nui," which incorporated what are now Kahoolawe, Molokai, and Lanai. Although the ocean has flowed in to create these four distinct islands, the channels between them are the shallowest, and the calmest, in Hawaii.

Because the tradewinds on Maui, like the rest of the state, blow consistently from the northeast, the island is much wetter on its north

When to visit

Although Maui's high season for tourism is mid-December to March, its climate remains fairly constant year-round, with temperatures generally hovering between the low seventies Fahrenheit (around 22°C) and the low eighties (around 28°C) in the daytime; at night the thermometer seldom reads below the low sixties (around 25°C). Warm clothing is only necessary if you plan to drive up to the summit of Haleakalā; at dawn, the most popular time to visit, temperatures regularly drop below freezing point. In principle the rainiest months are from December to February, but where you are on the island makes far more difference than what time of year it is, and the main leeward tourist areas seldom receive more than the occasional light shower even then.

Maui
AT A GLANCE

Lahaina

Once the capital of Hawaii and the rendezvous for the wild-living Pacific whaling fleet, Lahaina is the best place to get a sense of Maui's history.

▲ Lahaina Harbor

The central isthmus

The "neck" that connects Maui's two volcanoes is home to Kahului, the main commercial center; Pā'ia, a former plantation community turned surf-bum hang-out; and the faded but somehow appealing town of Wailuku, standing guard over the once-sacred 'Īao Valley.

Upcountry Maui

Upcountry Maui, on the lower, western slopes of Haleakalā, is an unexpected idyll; its cool green meadows and flower farms offer a pastoral escape from the bustle below.

▼ Upcountry Maui

▶ 'Īao Valley

IAO
NEEDLE
ELEV. 2250 FT

▲ Haleakalā Crater

Haleakalā Crater

Climb above the clouds to look out across the many-hued volcanic wasteland of vast Haleakalā Crater, or dwindle into cosmic insignificance by hiking down into it.

The road to Hāna

The countless waterfalls and ravines that line the tortuous, demanding road to Hāna, on the windward coasts of eastern Maui, make for a wonderful day-trip, culminating at lush 'Ohe'o Gulch.

▼ Little Beach, Mākena

◀ The road to Hāna

South Maui

According to the far from instinctive local usage, "South Maui" refers to the coastal resorts of Kīhei, Wailea and Mākena, along the southwest shoreline of eastern Maui. The further south you go here, the better the beaches you'll find.

Ideas

The big six

You'd have to stay on Maui a very long time to sample all it has to offer. As well as all that stupendous Polynesian scenery, it boasts superb tourist facilities, catering to every imaginable need and offering an extraordinary range of activities and opportunities. The sheer beauty of the place is probably what will stay with you longest; but if you're lucky enough to see a whale breaching, that may blot out everything else.

▲ The road to Hāna

However long you're going to spend on Maui, set aside at least a day to explore the wetter eastern side of the island; the scenery is out of this world.

P.123 ▶ THE ROAD TO HĀNA

▲ Surfing

Even if you don't learn the noble art of surfing while you're visiting its original home, you'll not be able to resist seeing how it's done.

P.125 ▶ THE ROAD TO HĀNA

▲ Haleakalā Crater

Large enough to comfortably hold Manhattan, what the ancient Hawiians called the "House of the Sun" has to be seen to be believed.

P.112 ▸ HALEAKALĀ

▼ Big Beach

Everyone's fantasy of the perfect Hawaiian beach: a huge stretch of golden sand pounded by awesome Pacific surf.

P.99 ▸ WAILEA AND MĀKENA

▲ The Feast at Lele

Forget the *lūʻaus*; pay a little extra, and enjoy some truly great food while you watch top-notch *hula* performers.

P.59 ▸ LAHAINA

▼ Whales

No matter how often you see them – and you will if you're here in winter – Maui's humpbacks remain utterly breathtaking.

P.56 ▸ LAHAINA

Scenic spots

Above all else, Maui is a natural wonderland, with magnificent landscapes on every side of the island as well, of course, as right on top. The finest scenery of all tends to be in areas where the rainfall is heavy enough to support rich green vegetation, which means you may well have to drive from your dry, sunny hotel to see it – but you certainly won't regret it.

▼ Haleakalā Crater

Hike into this extraordinary moonscape of craters and cinder cones at the top of Maui and you're a world away from the beaches and resorts below.

`P.112` ▸ HALEAKALĀ

▼ 'Ohe'o Gulch

Still widely – and spuriously – known as the Seven Sacred Pools, this tumbling sequence of waterfalls offers some great hiking.

`P.138` ▸ BEYOND HĀNA

▲ Kahakuloa Head

This towering highlight of the little-known Kahekili Highway guards a lovely traditional village.

P.69 ▶ NORTHWEST MAUI

▶ Wai'ānapanapa State Park

For coastal hiking, camping, and even cave-exploring, this gorgeous park in East Maui has no rival.

P.130 ▶ THE ROAD TO HĀNA

◀ 'Īao Valley

Beautiful 'Īao Valley is the highlight of any tour of central Maui.

P.84 ▶ CENTRAL MAUI

▼ Ke'anae Peninsula

There can be only one winner where the full force of the Pacific crashes endlessly against the palm-studded black lava of the Ke'anae Peninsula; and it's not the island.

P.127 ▶ THE ROAD TO HĀNA

Beaches

There are enough good beaches all over Maui that you shouldn't have to stray more than a mile or two from where you're staying in order to find one. Even so, half the fun of visiting the island is to keep searching for the "perfect" stretch of sand; and with so many to choose from, the quest is likely to be unending. In terms of areas, the shorelines of West and South Maui hold the best beaches – and by no coincidence, that's where nearly all the hotels are.

▲ Red Sand Beach

A short but dangerous hike leads to a genuine curio, a "pocket beach" of volcanic red sand that has its own strange beauty.

P.133 ▸ THE ROAD TO HĀNA

▲ Waiʻānapanapa Beach

Close to Hāna in remote East Maui, this gorgeous black-sand beach makes a superb spectacle, fringed with lush green palms and washed with white surf.

P.130 ▸ THE ROAD TO HĀNA

▶ Polo Beach

Though it's dominated by mighty resort hotels, this is still unquestionably Wailea's finest beach, drawing daily crowds from all over the island.

P.97 ▶ WAILEA AND MĀKENA

◀ Kā'anapali Beach

Perhaps the best family beach on Maui, this lovely golden strand stretches right in front of the hotels, restaurants, and stores of upscale Kā'anapali.

P.62 ▶ KĀ'ANAPALI

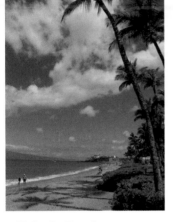

▼ Maluaka Beach

One of the loveliest spots to watch the sunset on Maui, and a great place to swim and snorkel, especially if you're staying at the adjacent *Maui Prince*.

P.99 ▶ WAILEA AND MĀKENA

▲ Big Beach

Though the mighty waves that slam the shores here make swimming dangerous, the strolling is idyllic, and the boogie-boarding is – for experts at least – irresistible.

P.99 ▶ WAILEA AND MĀKENA

Surfing and windsurfing

Maui holds some of the best surfing and windsurfing beaches in the world. However, anyone new to Hawaii, no matter how experienced elsewhere, should be sure to acclimatize at a few of the "lesser" spots before graduating to the challenging conditions of legendary places like Honolua Bay or Ho'okipa Beach. If you're looking to learn to surf or windsurf, then take lessons with a local; the gentle surf on Lahaina or Kīhei is ideal for beginners.

▲ Honomanū Bay

Fronted by a black-sand beach, this lush bay on the road to Hāna offers excellent surfing for those familiar with local conditions.

P.126 ▶ THE ROAD TO HĀNA

▼ Kanahā Beach

The best place to learn to windsurf on Maui, this throngs daily with eager sail-boarding students – and surfers too – keen to move on to awesome Ho'okipa.

P.74 ▶ KAHULUI

▲ Honolua Bay

At the northern tip of West Maui, the island's most popular destination for serious surfers makes a lovely setting even if you're only going to watch.

P.68 ▸ NORTHWEST MAUI

▶ Jaws

The supreme challenge for surfers; to get here at all you'll have to tackle several miles of red-dirt road, while to do battle with its stupendous waves takes a jet-ski tow-in.

P.125 ▸ THE ROAD TO HĀNA

◀ Māʻalaea Bay

This huge curving bay, protected by two volcanoes yet open to the Pacific winds, makes a wonderful playground for windsurfers from around the globe.

P.85 ▸ CENTRAL MAUI

▼ Hoʻokipa Beach

Commonly acknowledged as the world's best windsurfing spot, this central beach park plays host to major championships, and is also used by regular surfers.

P.123 ▸ THE ROAD TO HĀNA

Historic Maui

Maui's latest incarnation as a vacation playground is a recent development. The history of the island goes back a lot farther than that; some of the temples where ancient Hawaiians performed human sacrifices are still standing, while the nineteenth-century homes of missionaries and whaling captains give towns like Lahaina and Wailuku an added charm. You'll also come to realize how plantation laborers from all over the world gave modern Hawaii its cosmopolitan character.

▲ Hāna

Slow down your pace to enjoy a day or two in time-forgotten Hāna, a relic of how all Maui must have been before the advent of tourism.

P.130 ▶ THE ROAD TO HĀNA

▲ Alexander & Baldwin Sugar Museum

Learn about the nineteenth-century heyday of the sugar industry, and how immigrant laborers from all over the world combined to forge Maui's modern identity.

P.74 ▶ KAHULUI

▲ Lahaina

Once the capital of the Kingdom of Hawaii, and later a haven for roistering whaling crews, Lahaina remains Maui's prettiest old town, and still holds some lovely nineteenth-century buildings.

P.51 ▸ LAHAINA

▶ The Bailey House

The best historical museum on the island, focusing on the coming of the first Christian missionaries but also reflecting the heritage of the ancient Hawaiians.

P.77 ▸ WAILUKU

▼ Pi'ilanihale Heiau

What may well be the largest ancient Polynesian temple ever constructed stands in beautiful oceanfront gardens not far from Hāna.

P.128 ▸ THE ROAD TO HĀNA

Resort hotels

Maui and Lanai hold some of the world's most luxurious hotels. Enclaves like Kapalua and Kāʻanapali in West Maui, and Wailea and Mākena in South Maui can boast some truly extraordinary self-contained resorts, where sky-high room rates give guests access to utter luxury. Mere mortals can always venture in to dine at the restaurants and use other facilities, however, and no resort can stop outsiders from visiting the invariably superb adjoining beaches.

▼ Fairmont Kea Lani

Topped by gleaming white Moorish domes, the *Fairmont Kea Lani* in Wailea is a true fantasyland where you feel your every wish will be granted.

P.157 ▶ ACCOMMODATION

▼ The Four Seasons

Smart, elegant Wailea resort that's home to some great restaurants and amenities, and is right by a lovely beach.

P.157 ▶ ACCOMMODATION

▲ Hotel Hāna-Maui

Luxurious individual "cottages" are scattered across lawns that slope down the East Maui shoreline, facing the sunrise from the unspoiled town of Hāna.

P.159 ▶ ACCOMMODATION

◀ Mānele Bay Hotel

The quintessential Hawaiian resort hotel stands above the best beach on the so-called "private island" of Lanai.

P.160 ▶ ACCOMMODATION

▶ Hyatt Regency

With its waterslides and lagoons, and beach-front location, Kā'anapali's finest resort hotel is an opulent playground.

P.152 ▶ ACCOMMODATION

▼ Maui Prince

Mākena's only hotel enjoys a great oceanfront setting, with a splendid little beach and wonderful sunset views of Molokini.

P.157 ▶ ACCOMMODATION

Affordable accommodation

Visiting Maui doesn't have to cost the earth. The faded but atmospheric town of Wailuku holds a couple of inexpensive hostels, while there are genuinely affordable options to be found even in the major resort areas. The inns and hotels spotlighted here are by no means the cheapest of them all, but they're well-priced places that offer genuine charm and value for money.

▲ Banana Bungalow

Popular with international travelers, Wailuku's *Banana Bungalow* makes an ideal central base for cost-conscious visitors – they often offer free island excursions.

P.155 ▸ ACCOMMODATION

▼ Wailana Inn

Island-style motel rooms in northern Kīhei, much loved, not least for their bargain prices, by a predominantly gay clientele.

P.157 ▸ ACCOMMODATION

▲ Best Western Pioneer Inn

This characterful old inn has been at the epicenter of Lahaina's laidback social life for over a hundred years.

P.151 ▶ ACCOMMODATION

▶ The Mauian

Good rooms at great prices, right next to gorgeous Nāpili Beach in a friendly, family-run atmosphere – what more could you want?

P.154 ▶ ACCOMMODATION

▼ Northshore Hostel

This high standard of budget accommodation stands close to some good cheap restaurants in the heart of sleepy, charming Wailuku.

P.155 ▶ ACCOMMODATION

▲ Sunseeker Resort

Smart, well-priced (and gay-friendly) accommodation in a handy location at the northern end of Kīhei.

P.157 ▶ ACCOMMODATION

B&Bs

If you're one of those travelers who feels that giant resort hotels offer much too anonymous an experience, Maui has plenty of small-scale B&B alternatives. These don't necessarily cost less than a mid-range hotel or condo, but they have far more character, and usually come complete with a friendly owner or housekeeper who can provide advice on local attractions and activities. They can also be significantly more romantic than a hotel, if you're looking for an intimate getaway.

▲ Old Lahaina House

Very friendly B&B close to the heart of Lahaina, which offers good, bright rooms and even has its own pool.

P.152 ▸ ACCOMMODATION

▼ Old Wailuku Inn

Lovely historic home in Wailuku, handy for everywhere, with classy guest suites, taste-ful furnishings, and a welcoming feel.

P.155 ▸ ACCOMMODATION

▲ Heavenly Hāna Inn

Sophisticated Japanese-style B&B inn, just outside Hāna, with lovely fruit-filled gardens and a very relaxing ambience.

P.159 ▸ ACCOMMODATION

▸ Hale Hoʻokipa Inn

This appealing old island home, tucked away in Makawao in lovely Upcountry Maui, makes a wonderful escape from the resorts.

P.158 ▸ ACCOMMODATION

▾ Hāmoa Bay House and Bungalow

An utterly idyllic honeymoon hideaway, engulfed in the lush rainforest of East Maui.

P.159 ▸ ACCOMMODATION

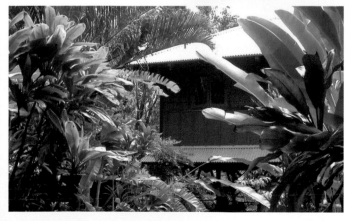

Hikes

Maui may not look that big on the map, and in places it can feel too over-developed for comfort, but there's still plenty of unspoiled wilderness out there if you're prepared to strap on a pair of hiking boots and leave the highway behind. Haleakalā is the ultimate test, but be sure also to take a hike into the rainforest at some point. Although East Maui is the obvious destination, the valleys and hillsides of West Maui also hold some fabulous trails within easy reach of the resorts.

▲ Sliding Sands Trail

It takes commitment and stamina to hike this grueling high-altitude trail, but you'll never forget its close-up views of the wonders of Haleakalā Crater.

P.117 ▶ HALEAKALĀ

▼ 'Ula'ino Road

Short, easy coastal hike that leads to a ravishing oceanfront waterfall-cum-grotto known as the Blue Pool.

P.129 ▶ THE ROAD TO HĀNA

▲ Waikamoi Nature Trail

Escape the crowds on the legendary road to Hāna by taking this tranquil little trail into the forests.

P.125 ▸ THE ROAD TO HĀNA

◀ Pīpīwai Trail

This fabulous rainforest hike passes through an eerie, dark bamboo grove en route to a remote waterfall high in Kīpahulu Valley.

P.139 ▸ BEYOND HĀNA

▼ Waiheʻe Ridge Trail

Climb as high as it's possible to go into the mountains of West Maui, to see lost swamps, uninhabited valleys, and breathtaking wild orchids.

P.80 ▸ WAILUKU

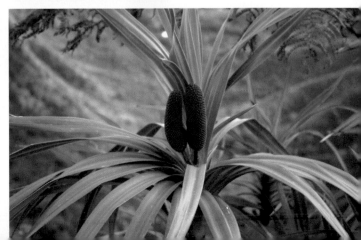

Tours and excursions

With so much to see on Maui, if you restrict yourself to places you can reach in your own vehicle you're likely to miss out on some of its most exciting attractions. Taking a helicopter trip is highly recommended, for a literal overview of the island, while it's also well worth taking a boat trip to see whales, to snorkel at little Molokini, or to cross over to neighboring Lanai. A guided bus tour isn't a bad idea even if you've rented a car; you might actually get to see more than the road ahead.

▲ Molokini

This tiny volcanic remnant, poking up from the Pacific off South Maui, makes a great destination for snorkeling or diving cruises.

P.170 ▶ ESSENTIALS

▲ Atlantis Submarines

Non-divers can admire Hawaii's wondrous marine life from the cabin of a real-life yellow submarine.

P.170 ▶ ESSENTIALS

▲ Helicopter flight

Get a bird's eye view of the whole island – you can even fly right over the top of Haleakalā – and you'll see enough beauty spots to keep you busy for the rest of your trip.

P.167 ▶ ESSENTIALS

▼ Lanai

Explore the so-called "private island" of Lanai on an eight-mile ferry trip from Lahaina.

P.142 ▶ LANAI

▲ Bus tour to Hāna

Letting someone else handle the twists and turns of driving the famed road to Hāna leaves you free to enjoy the sumptuous scenery.

P.123 ▶ THE ROAD TO HĀNA

▼ Whale watching

In winter, the waters off Maui are alive with frolicking humpback whales; watch them from the beach, or take a cruise to see them up close.

P.56 ▶ LAHAINA

Kids' Maui

If the weather stays fine for your whole vacation, then you shouldn't find much problem keeping the kids happy. Quite apart from the various activities and beaches listed elsewhere in this book, Maui does also hold some fun attractions for kids, with the aquarium at the Maui Ocean Center top among them.

▲ Whale Museum

This little museum, perched above the stores in central Kā'anapali, brings the fascinating world of the whalers to life.

P.62 ▸ KĀ'ANAPALI

▲ Waterslides

What child could resist the intricate labyrinths of tunnels and waterslides to be found at hotels like Kā'anapali's *Westin Maui*?

P.153 ▸ ACCOMMODATION

▲ Maui Ocean Center

This top-quality aquarium is the perfect rainy-day destination, providing a chance to learn all about the colorful denizens of the Hawaiian deep.

P.86 ▸ CENTRAL MAUI

▸ Kā'anapali Beach

Pretty much any beach on Maui will delight the kids, but Kā'anapali is probably the best for convenience and safety as well as soft sand.

P.62 ▸ KĀ'ANAPALI

▾ The Sugar Cane Train

A perfect little day-trip in West Maui; ride the plantation railroad from historic Lahaina to the beach at Kā'anapali.

P.168 ▸ ESSENTIALS

Gourmet restaurants

Maui is blessed with an abundance of truly excellent restaurants; the five selections here just skim the surface. The most distinctive feature of island cuisine has been the emergence of something loosely known as "Hawaiian Regional" or "new Hawaiian" food, which closely resembles what may be familiar as Pacific Rim cooking. Features include cooking fresh fish to accentuate its delicate flavors, and complementing dishes with Asian herbs and spices.

▲ Spago

In this ultra-glamorous resort restaurant, beautifully poised at the *Four Seasons*, Wolfgang Puck pulls out all the stops to deliver superb Pacific-Rim dishes.

P.104 ▶ WAILEA AND MĀKENA

▼ Roy's

Roy Yamaguchi is a pioneer of modern Hawaiian cooking; both his Maui restaurants, at Kahana and Kīhei, serve truly delicious food.

PP.70 & 95 ▶ NORTHWEST MAUI & KĪHEI

▲ Haili'imaile General Store

Far from the resorts, and housed in a former grocery store, this Upcountry restaurant thrives on the reputation of a great and ever-changing Asian-flavored menu.

P.111 ▸ UPCOUNTRY MAUI

▼ Sansei

With two locations, in Kapalua and Kīhei, *Sansei* serves up the best Japanese-style fish on the island, at surprisingly reasonable prices.

PP.70 & 96 ▸ NORTHWEST MAUI & KĪHEI

▸ Hotel Hāna-Maui

The atmospheric terrace setting and laid-back ambience of the dining room at the *Hotel Hāna-Maui* is matched by the excellence of its inventive Pacific-Rim cuisine.

P.134 ▸ THE ROAD TO HĀNA

Casual eating

Not every meal on Maui can be a gourmet extravaganza; you'll also find plenty of straightforward restaurants that serve good food at affordable prices. Enough tourists are out exploring the island every day that high-quality cafés flourish almost everywhere, while all the fresh fruit and other island produce means that even roadside stalls offer surprisingly tasty snacks to passing travelers.

▲ AK's Café

Good, healthy food in Central Maui; a convenient stop-off for a quick meal as you tour the island.

P.82 ▸ WAILUKU

▲ Nāhiku Fruit Stand

One of the true highlights along the road to Hāna; delicious juices, smoothies and snacks, with an excellent barbecue place alongside.

P.134 ▸ THE ROAD TO HĀNA

▼ SeaWatch

In the evening, this South Maui golf-course restaurant is a pricey option, but lunch is a real bargain – and the views are out of this world.

P.103 ▸ WAILEA AND MĀKENA

▲ Soup Nutz and Java Jazz

Funky, friendly cafe in West Maui; relax over an early coffee, or enjoy some jazz in the evening.

P.71 ▸ NORTHWEST MAUI

▼ Penne Pasta

This popular, ever-expanding pizza and pasta joint offers Lahaina's best value for a tasty meal.

P.60 ▸ LAHAINA

Food and drink

Although it has to be acknowledged that Hawaii belongs to the United States, and you can therefore find pretty much any fast food on Maui that you'd expect to find on the mainland, there's still plenty that's distinctively Hawaiian. The best place to sample traditional foods like *kālua* pork is at a commercial *lū'au*, while the favorite dishes introduced to the island by generations of immigrants feature on the menus of "local" diners all over Maui.

▲ Cocktails

Why come all the way to Hawaii unless it's to drink a Mai Tai at sunset with a paper parasol poking from the glass?

P.104 ▸ WAILEA AND MĀKENA

▲ Saimin

If Hawaii has a national dish these days, it's *saimin*, or noodle soup; you can buy a bowl for under $5 in cafés all over the island.

P.111 ▸ UPCOUNTRY MAUI

▼ Fish in a fancy restaurant

The chefs of Maui are renowned for their inventive ways with fish; be sure to try *opah* (moonfish) or *moi* (threadfish) at one of the island's top restaurants.

P.64 ▶ KĀ'ANAPALI

▲ Fruit stands

Maui's abundance of succulent fresh fruit means that roadside shacks practically give the stuff away.

P.134 ▶ THE ROAD TO HĀNA

▼ Kālua pork at a lū'au

Baked all day in an underground oven, shredded *kālua* pork, reminiscent of Southern barbecued hog, is a highlight of Maui's *lū'aus*.

P.59 ▶ LAHAINA

▲ Poi

The authentic taste of old Hawaii; you have to try this purple taro-root paste at least once, even if you agree with Captain Cook that it's a "disagreeable mess."

P.166 ▶ ESSENTIALS

Flora and fauna

Hawaii is a unique ecological laboratory. Not only are the islands isolated by a "moat" at least two thousand miles wide in every direction, but having emerged from the sea as lifeless lumps of lava, they were never populated by the diversity of species that spread across the rest of the planet. That means Maui is still home to its own unique ecosystem, featuring plants, birds, and insects found nowhere else on earth.

▲ Gardens

Gardens all over the island are open to the public, giving visitors the chance to see and buy blossoms seldom encountered in the wild.

P.107 ▶ UPCOUNTRY MAUI

▼ Birds

Maui is home to some of the rarest birds on the planet, with differing habitats that support an extraordinary range of species.

P.126 ▶ THE ROAD TO HĀNA

▼ Protea

The farms of Upcountry Maui are renowned for their multi-colored protea blooms, a perfect touch of color to take home.

P.105 ▸ UPCOUNTRY MAUI

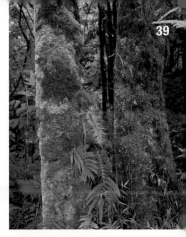

▲ The rainforest

Even if you spend most of your vacation in the sun, be sure to venture down at least one of the many trails that penetrate the lush heart of Maui's rainforest.

P.138 ▸ BEYOND HĀNA

▼ Orchids

Whether growing wild in remote valleys and hillsides, or carefully cultivated in commercial gardens, Maui's iridescent orchids are an unfailing delight.

P.123 ▸ THE ROAD TO HĀNA

▲ Silverswords

The rare and delicate silversword plant, found only on the highest slopes of Hawaii's volcanoes, makes a ravishing spectacle even if you don't get to see its once-in-a-lifetime flowering.

P.120 ▸ HALEAKALĀ

Shows and nightlife

Maui's nightlife, it has to be admitted, is relatively sedate; there just doesn't seem to be a large enough local population for clubs or other nightspots to cater to a regular clientele. Instead, most of the entertainment on offer is firmly directed at tourists, and often panders to preconceptions of what Polynesia "ought" to be like rather than how Hawaii actually is. That said, *lū'aus* can be great fun even if they're not "authentic," and with luck you'll get to hear some great Hawaiian music too.

▲ Drums of the Pacific

If Hawaiian-style entertainment is more important to you than the food, you'll enjoy the show at this Kā'anapali *lū'au*.

P.65 ▶ KĀ'ANAPALI

▲ The Feast at Lele

A fantastic setting, superb and unusual food, and a great show – not a *lū'au* exactly, but the best night out on Maui.

P.59 ▸ LAHAINA

▶ Slack key night at the Ritz Carlton

Superb Hawaiian music, performed by the very top masters of the genre in a somewhat austere setting that's transformed by the joy of artists and audience alike.

P.71 ▸ NORTHWEST MAUI

▼ Old Lahaina Lū'au

The island's finest *lū'au*, in a spacious ocean-front location in Lahaina, and offering an authentic taste of traditional Hawaiian *hula*.

P.60 ▸ LAHAINA

Ocean fun

The scope for enjoying yourself in the sea off Maui is virtually infinite. Take some basic precautions, like informing yourself of local beach conditions – ask a lifeguard, or someone at your hotel, or read this book – protect yourself against the sun, and get on with it. Surfing and windsurfing are summarized on p.16, but there are plenty of activities that don't require that level of expertise.

▲ Diving

Hawaii's warm Pacific waters are home to swarms of colorful fish, making Maui a paradise for divers.

P.169 ▸ ESSENTIALS

▼ Boogie-boarding

Much of the thrill of surfing, with little of the effort; many resort beaches offer ideal conditions for first-time boogie-boarders.

P.136 ▶ BEYOND HĀNA

▲ Kayaking

Ocean kayaking, especially along the shorelines of South and West Maui, is rewarding and exhilarating.

P.101 ▶ WAILEA AND MĀKENA

▲ Snorkeling

Exploring the nooks and crannies of Maui's coast with a mask and fins can be endlessly fascinating – and equipment rental is available everywhere.

P.62 ▶ KĀ'ANAPALI

▼ Swimming

You don't need a reservation, you don't need fancy equipment, and you don't have to pay anyone; just get in the water and go.

P.97 ▶ WAILEA AND MĀKENA

Outdoor activities

Think of something you like doing outdoors, and you can bet someone on Maui has set up a business that will let you do it (well, maybe not that). Maui is renowned among the Hawaiian islands as attracting the most active visitors – the ones who want to ride things, jump off things, and generally rush around enjoying themselves – and you'll be given every opportunity to join in.

▼ Skyline

A new and adventurous option in the Upcountry woodlands – a daredevil course of aerial ziplines.

P.108 ▶ UPCOUNTRY MAUI

▲ Golf

Maui's meticulously groomed resort golf courses are among the very finest on the planet.

P.97 ▸ WAILEA AND MĀKENA

▼ Hang-gliding

Get closer to heaven by soaring on the thermal air currents above beautiful Upcountry Maui.

P.107 ▸ UPCOUNTRY MAUI

◀ Downhill biking

The ultimate in leisure travel; after being driven to the top of Haleakalā at dawn, you simply roll back down again, and barely have to nudge a pedal.

P.112 ▸ HALEAKALĀ

▼ Horse riding

Opportunities for horse riding can be found all over Maui, from guided trips through Haleakalā Crater to galloping through remote meadows.

P.172 ▸ ESSENTIALS

Shopping and souvenirs

While not on par with Honolulu as a shopping destination, Maui does hold plenty of malls, stores, and shopping streets. As well as all those ephemeral needs you suddenly encounter on a tropical holiday – sunhats, swimming costumes, aloha shirts – it also offers abundant souvenirs to show the folks back home what they were missing. And some of the crafts are even worth buying for yourself.

▲ Leis

You'll know you're in Hawaii when you're garlanded with your first flower lei; why not take one home to your friends and family?

P.176 ▶ ESSENTIALS

▼ Aloha wear

Yes, everyone really does wear Hawaiian shirts in Hawaii; and before you know it you'll find yourself wearing one too.

P.81 ▶ WAILUKU

▲ Hawaiian music

Few first-time visitors leave Maui without a new-found love for Hawaiian music; be sure to pick up that Israel Kamakawiwo'ole or Hapa CD while you still can.

P.94 ▶ KĪHEI

◄ Hula crafts

If you want to buy something truly Hawaiian, how about the various artefacts you'll see used in *hula* performances, like a decorated gourd or a feathered rattle?

P.88 ▶ CENTRAL MAUI

▼ Tiki products

You'll be needing a few *hula* dolls, *tiki* carvings, and cocktail accessories for that Hawaiian theme bar you're going to build in your basement.

P.88 ▶ CENTRAL MAUI

Places

Lahaina

Lahaina, the only true town in West Maui, is one of the prettiest communities in all Hawaii. Timber-frame buildings line its main oceanfront street; yachts bob in the harbor; coconut palms sway to either side of the central banyan tree; surfers swirl into the thin fringe of beach to the south; and the mountains of West Maui dominate the skyline. Its instant appeal lures a fair number of visitors, and at times it can be unpleasantly crowded, but even so, Lahaina is unquestionably an attractive base. Early evening is especially unforgettable, with the sun casting a rich glow on the mountains as it sets behind the island of Lanai.

Banyan Tree Square

At the very heart of Lahaina, Banyan Tree Square is a pretty public space that's often rendered a little too busy for comfort by large influxes

▼ BANYAN TREE SQUARE

of tourists. The magnificent banyan tree that almost completely fills it was planted in 1873, and consists of at least twenty trunks. Chirruping birds congregate in the branches, while portrait artists tout for customers in the shade below.

Here and there on the surrounding lawns, outlines mark the former extent of Lahaina Fort, built in 1832 and demolished in 1854. One small corner of its walls, which once held 47 cannons, has been reconstructed, at the southwest end of the square.

Court House

The stolid, four-square Court House dates from 1859.

Lahaina's past

There's little left to show for it nowadays, but Lahaina boasts a colorful past. Kamehameha the Great spent a year here preparing for what was to be an unsuccessful invasion of Kauai, while his successors, Kamehamehas II and III, ruled from Lahaina between the 1820s and 1840s. Over the following decades hard-bitten whaling crews jostled with missionaries in a rip-roaring frontier town once described as "one of the breathing holes of Hell." Lahaina spent most of the twentieth century as a sleepy sugar town – its mill eventually closed in 1999 – and only turned into the hectic tourist destination of today after the emergence of the resort development at neighboring Kāʻanapali during the 1970s.

LAHAINA

Railroad Depot

Lahaina Center

Pioneer Mill

Pioneer Mill

Lahaina Shopping Center

Old Lahaina Center

Wo Hing Temple

Old Lahaina Book Emporium

Maria Lanakila Church

CAFÉS & RESTAURANTS

Buns of Maui	2
Cheeseburger in Paradise	9
David Paul's Lahaina Grill	7
Down to Earth	4
Erik's Seafood Grotto	3
The Feast at Lele	13
Gerard's	6
Lahaina Coolers	11
Lahaina Fish Co	8
Lemongrass	1
Moose McGillycuddy's	
Pacific 'O	13
Penne Pasta	10
Sunrise Café	12

Baldwin Home

Lahaina Public Library

Wharf Cinema Center

Hale Pa'ahao

Banyan Tree Square

Court House

Lahaina Harbor

Lahaina Beach

Waine'e Church

Shaw Street

505 Front Street Mall

Mala Ulu Olele Park

N

0   Yards   250

ACCOMMODATION

Best Western Pioneer Inn	D
Lahaina Inn	A
Lahaina Shores Beach Resort	E
Ohana Maui Islander	C
Old Lahaina House	F
Plantation Inn	B

Downstairs, you'll find the small local visitor center, as well as the Banyan Tree Gallery, which hosts interesting, free art exhibitions (daily 9am–5pm). Up on the second floor, the town's former courtroom, last used in 1987, now serves as the Lahaina Heritage Center (daily 10am–4pm; $1 suggested donation), where displays on local history focus especially on the whaling era.

The Pioneer Inn

The *Pioneer Inn* has, since it was moved from the island of Lanai in 1901, been the main social center of Lahaina. Its original owner, a Canadian Mountie who had pursued a criminal all the way to Maui, decided to stay on and go into the hotel business. Still a hotel – see p.151 – it makes an atmospheric place to stop in for a beer.

Lahaina Public Library

Lahaina Public Library stands on the site of a royal taro patch, personally tended by the first three Kamehamehas. Bricks set into the grass on its seaward side trace the foundations of the Brick Palace, Hawaii's first Western-style building, which was built for Kamehameha the Great in 1798 by an English convict who had managed to escape from Australia.

Lahaina Harbor

A simple, modern white structure has replaced what was the oldest Pacific lighthouse, built to serve the whaling fleet in 1840. Shielded by a breakwater of boulders, Lahaina Harbor now serves as an overworked pleasure-boat marina, and is also the base for ferries to Lanai and Molokai. Although the harbor wall has kiosks for most local boat operators, it's not much of an area to stroll around, and you can usually get better prices for trips from the activity centers along Front Street.

Lahaina Beach

Lahaina Beach, with its shallow water, sandy bottom, and gentle breaks, is where companies such as the Goofy Foot Surf School (☎808/244-9283, ⓦwww.goofyfootsurfschool.com) and the Nancy Emerson School of Surfing (☎808/244-7873, ⓦwww.surfclinics.com) teach their clients the rudiments of surfing, and beginners and old-timers alike swoop back and forth. The beach itself is too narrow for long days of family fun, but it's fine for a stroll.

The Baldwin Home

Front Street just north of Banyan Tree Square ☎808/661-3262. Daily 10am–4pm. $3, $5 per couple or family.

The Baldwin Home is Lahaina's oldest surviving building. Dating from the days when this was Hawaii's royal capital, it was the Maui base of the Sandwich Islands Mission and is now a reasonably interesting museum of missionary and local history. The admission price includes a brief narrated tour, after which visitors are free to take a closer look around.

Constructed in 1834, with 24-inch-thick walls of plastered lava and coral, the house is named for Reverend Dwight Baldwin, who took it over three years later. Baldwin remained as pastor of Lahaina's Waine'e Church until 1871, and much of his original furniture is still in place. Oddly frivolous touches among the chairs, quilts, and memorabilia include an inlaid *koa* gaming table, and a table-top croquet set. On one wall hangs a "Native Doctor's License" from 1865, with a scale of charges ranging from $50 down to $10, according to whether the patient had a "Very great sickness," "Less

▼ LAHAINA HARBOR

▲ THE BALDWIN HOME

than that," "A Good Deal Less," a "Small sickness," or a "Very Small."

Wo Hing Temple

Daily 10am–4pm. $1. The distinguished-looking building with the unmistakably Oriental facade was built in 1912 as the meeting place for the Wo Hing Society, a mutual-aid organization established in China during the seventeenth century. Until the 1970s, the Wo Hing Temple housed elderly members of the society, but it's now an intriguing little museum devoted to the Chinese immigration to Hawaii, with a small Taoist altar on its second story.

Amid the faded signs and battered pots and pans in the decrepit adjacent cookhouse, you can watch scratchy film footage shot by Thomas Edison in Hawaii in 1898 and 1906. Shown in a continuous loop, it offers fascinating glimpses of Waikīkī before the tourists arrive, and plantation life before trucks replaced horses.

Waine'e Church

The first church on Maui, built in 1828 after five years of open-air services, was Waine'e Church, one block back from the sea. Twice destroyed by hurricanes, and burned down in 1894 during protests against the overthrow of the Hawaiian monarchy, this less-than-enthralling edifice has been officially known as Waiola Church since it was last rebuilt in 1953.

Tombs in the sun-scorched graveyard alongside, however, include some of the greatest names in early Hawaiian history. A simple monument commemorates the last king of Kauai, Kaumuali'i, who was buried here in 1825 after being kidnapped and forced to live in exile. Nearby are Queen Keopuolani, one of the many wives of Kamehameha the Great, who was of such distinguished blood that her husband could only enter her presence naked on all fours; the governor of Maui, Hoapili Kane, who died in 1840; and his widow and successor, Hoapili Wahine.

Lahainaluna

High above Lahaina town, reached by a winding two-mile climb up Lahainaluna Road past the Pioneer Sugar Mill, Lahainaluna Seminary was founded by American missionaries in 1831. Its goal was to teach Hawaiians to read and write, in the hope of producing future teachers and ministers. In 1850, the seminary passed into government control, and it eventually became Hawaii's most prestigious public high school. During the Gold Rush years many Californians sent their children here rather than risk the long journey East.

Visitors are welcome to take a look around the high school grounds; identify yourself at the gate first. The only building you can enter is the seminary's small printing house, Hale Pa'i

(Mon–Fri by appointment only; free; ☎808/661-3262). Dating from 1837, it holds some of Hawaii's first printed books, as well as a replica of the press that produced them.

Among the seminary's earliest pupils were Hawaii's most famous native historians, Samuel Kamakau and David Malo. Malo had been brought up at the court of Kamehameha the Great on the Big Island and was 38 when he first came here. Although he became a Christian, and was a minister at the old village of Kalepolepo in what's now Kīhei, he was also a passionate defender of the rights of the Hawaiian people. Before he died in 1853, he asked to be buried "beyond the rising tide of the foreign invasion." His gravesite, above Lahainaluna at Puʻu Paʻupaʻu, is marked with a huge letter "L" (for Lahainaluna) etched into the hillside and visible from all over Lahaina.

Launiupoko State Wayside Park

Three miles south out of Lahaina.
With its coconut palms leaning out from the shoreline and larger trees shading the tables on the lawn, Launiupoko State Wayside Park is an attractive place to picnic; the only snag is that it's very much in earshot of the highway. From the center of the park, boulder walls curve out to enclose a shallow artificial pool, suitable for small children, with two narrow outlets to the sea. South of that is a small beach of gritty sand, while to the north the lava rocks create a sea wall, alive with scuttling black crabs. The gentle surf here makes the offshore waters a good place for apprentice surfers. The park offers showers and restrooms, but camping is forbidden.

Olowalu

Six miles south of Lahaina. There's little more to Olowalu than

PLACES | Lahaina

The Olowalu Massacre

Olowalu was the site of the worst massacre in Hawaiian history, perpetrated by Captain Simon Metcalfe of the American merchant ship *Eleanora* in 1790. After Hawaiians had killed a member of his crew off East Maui, Metcalfe sailed for Olowalu, which he was told was the home of the chief culprit. Offering to continue trading, he lured more than two hundred canoes out to the *Eleanora*, then bombarded them with his seven cannons. More than a hundred Hawaiians died.

Captain Metcalfe's 18-year-old son, Thomas, was to pay for his father's sins. Metcalfe had previously antagonized a Big Island chief, Kameʻeiamoku, who vowed to kill the next white man he met. Ignorant of events at Olowalu, Thomas Metcalfe landed at Kawaihae on the Big Island a few days later and was killed when Kameʻeiamoku attacked his six-man schooner *Fair American*. Only Isaac Davis of its crew was spared, for putting up such valiant resistance.

When the *Eleanora* arrived at Kawaihae in search of the younger Metcalfe, first mate John Young was sent ashore to investigate. After Kamehameha the Great himself prevented Young from rejoining his vessel, Captain Metcalfe concluded that his envoy had been killed and sailed away. Davis and Young remained on the islands for the rest of their lives. They were responsible for teaching the Hawaiians to fight with muskets and cannons – the royal arsenal began with two guns seized from the *Fair American* – and personally directed Kamehameha's armies in major battles during his conquest of all the Hawaiian islands.

a tiny row of stores *mauka* (inland) of the highway, which includes the restaurant *Chez Paul* (see p.58). Although there's no public access to the ocean, you can take a short hike towards the mountains to a cluster of ancient petroglyphs. Head round to the left behind the stores and then continue inland, following the dirt road that starts immediately left of a water tower. After ten minutes' walk through the cane fields, you reach a cinder cone from which one side has sheared off, leaving a flat wall of red rock. Railings a few feet up the rock mark the site of the petroglyphs, but the stairs and walkways that once enabled visitors to climb up to them have largely vanished. So too have many of the petroglyphs, while others have been vandalized. However, you should still spot several wedge-shaped human figures etched into the rock, together with a sailing canoe or two, characterized by their "crab-claw" sails.

Ukemehame and Pāpalaua

South of Olowalu, the cane fields come to an end, and Hwy-30 skirts the shoreline only a few feet above sea level. It's possible to park just about anywhere, and during the winter whale-watching season that's exactly what people do – often with very little warning.

Ukemehame Beach County Park, three miles along, consists of a very small area of lawn between the highway and the ocean, with picnic tables and a couple of portable rest rooms, fringed by a small strip of sand. It's all a bit exposed to the road, as although lots of trees have been planted, they remain very short. By this point, the mountains that rise just inland of the road are much drier and barer than further north.

Pāpalaua State Wayside, leading south from Ukemehame, is a long dirt strip used as a parking lot, separated from the sand by a thin line of scrubby trees. Local surfers and snorkelers – snorkeling is best around the rocks beyond the south end of the beach – set up tents, but there are virtually no facilities.

Papawai Point

Immediately beyond Pāpalaua, the highway starts its climb over (and through) the headland of Papawai Point. The roadside lookout here, which commands views across to Kahoolawe, Lanai, and East Maui, makes one of Maui's best whale-watching sites, but it can also cause traffic congestion in winter.

The Lahaina Pali Trail

Until the hard labor of convicts constructed the first road around

▲ LAHAINA PALI TRAIL

the southern coast of West Maui, in 1900, the only way to reach Lahaina via dry land was to follow the centuries-old *alaloa*, or "long road," across the mountains. A five-mile stretch is now open as the Lahaina Pali Trail – a grueling hike that climbs 1600 feet above sea level and, being situated at the dry, exposed southern tip of the island, is also a very hot one. Don't expect to penetrate the mysterious green heart of the interior; for that, the Waiheʻe Ridge Trail (see p.80) is a better bet. Your rewards instead will be the sight of some ravishing upland meadows, carpeted with magnificent purple, yellow, and red flowers, and expansive views out to the islands of Lanai and Kahoolawe and down across the isthmus.

▲ OLD LAHAINA BOOK EMPORIUM

Both ends of the trail are a long way from the nearest town, so you'll need a car to reach either trailhead. Unless you can arrange to be picked up at the far end, hiking its full length necessitates a ten-mile round trip. The path leaves Honoapiʻilani Highway from a parking lot near the 11-mile marker at Ukemehame and rejoins it five miles south of Wailuku, immediately south of the white bridge that lies between its intersections with highways 31 (to Kihei) and 380 (to Kahului). Whichever end you start – the eastern slope is the steeper – you'll have at least a mile of stiff climbing before the trail levels out, still far below the mountain tops. The trail then meanders through successive gulches to cross Kealaloloa Ridge, with almost the only shade being provided by the occasional native dryland sandalwood tree.

Shops

Lahaina Cannery Mall

North end of Lahaina near Mala Wharf. As well as Long's Drugs and Safeways for staple supplies, this largely indoor mall offers a good food court, and souvenir stores ranging from tacky T-shirt places to the upscale Lahaina Printsellers with its antique and reproduction maps and prints.

Lahaina Center

Three blocks north of Banyan Tree Square. The Lahaina Center mall has never quite filled up, but it does hold some large clothing outlets, including aloha-wear specialists Hilo Hattie, and also features its own reproduction Hawaiian village, the Hale Kahiko, which stages *hula* shows and is open for explanatory tours (daily 11am–4pm).

Old Lahaina Book Emporium

834 Front St ☎ 808/661-1399. Despite the address, Maui's best used bookstore is actually tucked slightly back from Front Street, but it's well worth tracking down, for a great selection of Hawaii-related books and much more besides.

Cafés

Buns of Maui

878 Front St ☎808/661-5407.
Tucked away just behind
Front Street, this appealing
little bakery serves fresh
pastries, muffins, and, of course,
sumptuous cinnamon buns
along with its coffees in the
morning, and switches to
sandwiches later on.

Restaurants

Cheeseburger in Paradise

811 Front St ☎808/661-4855. Busy,
crowded seafront restaurant,
perched on stilts above the
water and open for all meals
daily. The great views, buzzing
ambience, and seafaring bric-
a-brac are more of a draw
than the food, which is very
much what the name suggests,
though in addition to meaty
cheeseburgers ($8–10) they have
fish sandwiches and tofu nut-
burgers at similar prices. There's
live music nightly.

Chez Paul

Olowalu Village, Olowalu ☎808/661-
3843. Dinner only, with two seatings,
at 6.30pm and 8.30pm. Closed Sun.
Incongruous and very expensive
French bistro, set behind a
pretty little brick wall just off
the highway six miles south of
Lahaina. Most of the appetizers
cost at least $10, though there's
caviar for $66, while entrees
such as seafood *bouillabaisse* and
Tahitian duck are well over $30.

David Paul's Lahaina Grill

Lahaina Inn, 127 Lahainaluna Rd
☎808/667-5117. Upmarket,
dinner-only restaurant serving
some of Maui's finest Pacific
Rim cuisine, just off Front
Street in downtown
Lahaina. The setting
is slightly cramped
and unatmospheric,
but the food is
excellent. Of the
appetizers, try the
superb Kona lobster
crabcake ($17) or
the succulent deep-
fried oysters. Entrees
include rack of lamb
flavored with coffee
($39), *kālua* duck
($29), and various
fish dishes, while the
fruity desserts are
wonderful. A five-
course tasting menu
costs $74.

Down to Earth

193 Lahainaluna Rd
☎808/667-2855.
Mon–Sat 7.30am–9pm,
Sun 8.30am–8pm. A

▼ CHEESEBURGER IN PARADISE

downtown organic food store where the hot and cold buffets at the deli counter sell a copious array of mainly vegan dishes by the pound – a true bargain. There's minimal seating both indoors and outside.

Erik's Seafood Grotto

843 Waine'e St ☎808/662-8780. Smart seafood-joint-cum-nightclub, tucked away in the central Old Lahaina Shopping Center, that serves $10 fish'n'chips, pastas, and sandwiches for weekday lunches, and fancier seafood entrees like baked stuffed prawns, or seafood stews like *cioppino* or *bouillabaisse*, for around $30 in the evening. There's also a sushi and sashimi bar, where prices drop by half towards the end of the evening. Open-mic or DJ entertainment are often on offer after hours at weekends.

The Feast at Lele

505 Front St ☎808/667-5353 or 1-866/244-5353, ⊛www .feastatlele.com. April–Sept daily 6pm, Oct–March daily 5.30pm; schedule may vary. An inspired cross between a *lū'au* and a gourmet restaurant that, for once, lavishes as much care on the food as on the entertainment. Among the Polynesian specialties are *kālua* pork from Hawaii, *fafa* (steamed chicken) and *e'iota* (marinated raw fish) from Tahiti, and grilled fish in banana leaves from Samoa. Each of the excellent and unusual five courses consists of at least two dishes, while the very romantic beachfront setting has individual tables set out facing the ocean at sunset. Music and *hula* performances punctuate the evening, culminating in a Samoan fire dance. Though steep, the $99 adult charge includes

unlimited cocktails and other beverages; for children, it's $69. Reservations are essential.

Gerard's

Plantation Inn, 174 Lahainaluna Rd ☎808/661-8939. This upscale dinner-only restaurant adds a Hawaiian twist to traditional French cuisine, to create a menu of appetizers ($10–25) such as snails with wild mushrooms or foie gras with truffles, and entrees (up to $40) like veal sweetbreads, or *opakapaka* (snapper). Desserts include profiteroles and other classic pastries.

Lahaina Coolers

180 Dickenson St ☎808/661-7082. Central bistro serving eggy breakfasts, then an extensive menu of salads, pastas, pizzas, tortillas, steaks, and fresh Hawaiian fish, priced at $12–22, for lunch and dinner. A couple of blocks from the sea, but it's open and breezy, with a pleasant atmosphere.

Lahaina Fish Co

831 Front St, Lahaina ☎808/661-3472. High-quality seafood restaurant, poised on a beautiful *lānai* that juts out over the ocean. Hawaiian fish entrees ($22–26) are available broiled, grilled, or blackened Cajun-style, while a raw bar serves clams and oysters on the half-shell for around $10 and fresh sashimi for $13. Devout carnivores can stick to steak, chicken, or ribs.

Lemongrass

930 Waine'e St, Lahaina ☎808/667-6888. Bright little Vietnamese/Thai restaurant, behind the Lahaina Center. In addition to soups and noodle dishes such as beef *phó* ($7) and pad Thai with shrimp or

▲ PACIFIC 'O

chicken ($10), there's a full menu of meat and seafood entrees, including plenty of curries, almost all under $14.

Moose McGillycuddy's

844 Front St ☎808/667-7758. Hectic restaurant-cum-nightclub that starts the day with cheap breakfasts ($2 specials between 7.30am and 8.30am only, plus twenty different omelets at $8); follows up with standard lunches and dinners of burgers, sandwiches, pastas, and steaks; and tops things off with live music and/or dancing nightly 9.30pm–2am ($2 cover charge).

Pacific 'O

505 Front St ☎808/667-4341. Attractive oceanfront mall restaurant, serving Pacific Rim cuisine on a beach-level terrace with indoor dining above. The relatively simple lunch specials ($10–15) include a bleu cheese burger, a chicken wrap, and delicious sesame fish. In the evening, try appetizers ($9–12) such as the shrimp won tons in Hawaiian salsa, and entrees like "Thai dye duck" – a coconut curry ($25) – or tempura blocks of fish ($29). For vegetarians,

the "leaning tower of tofu" costs $13.50 at lunch, $24 for dinner. Leave room for the huge, delicious chocolate desserts. Live jazz Fri & Sat from 9pm.

Penne Pasta

180 Dickenson St ☎808/661-6633. Cheerful Italian café, with sidewalk and indoor seating, serving straightforward but tasty pastas, salads, and pizzas for under $10. The thin, crispy flatbread topped with olives, capers, basil, oregano, and roasted peppers is particularly good. Lunch is served on weekdays only.

Sunrise Café

693A Front St at Market St ☎808/661-8558. Small, laid-back, and very central café-cum-restaurant, with outdoor seating beside its own tiny patch of beach. Coffees, smoothies, and full cooked breakfasts are served from dawn onwards, plus $6–9 sandwiches, plate lunches, and salads later on. No credit cards.

Shows

Old Lahaina Lū'au

Lahaina Cannery Mall, 1251 Front

St ☎808/667-1998 or 1-800/248-5828, 🌐www.oldlahainaluau.com. April–Sept daily 5.45pm, Oct–March daily 5.15pm. $85, ages 12 and under $55. Maui's best *lū'au* shows its rivals how a *lū'au* really should be done. The spacious oceanfront location is ideal, enabling guests to explore the various displays and crafts stalls and watch the sunset before they're seated to enjoy a full meal of traditional foods like *kālua* pork, *poi*, and *lau lau*. The evening culminates with a skilfully staged show that traces the history of *hula*. Ticket prices include an open cocktail bar.

'Ulalena

Lahaina Center, 900 Front St ☎808/661-9913, 🌐www.ulalena .com. Mon–Sat 5pm. $48–68, under-13s $28–45. Somewhat ersatz but undeniably spectacular musical show, which tells a simplified story of ancient Hawaii through exclusively Hawaiian-language songs. It's a little hard to follow if you're not familiar with the material, while if you are, you may well prefer something more authentic.

Warren and Annabelle's Magic Show

Lahaina Center, 900 Front St ☎808/667-6244, 🌐www .warrenandannabelles.com. Tues–Sat 6.30pm. Adults only, $45, or $80 with food and two cocktails. Although there's nothing particularly Hawaiian about this entertaining magic show, for a fun night out it's unbeatable. Each group of guests must solve a puzzle to gain admission to the pre-show bar, where cocktails and a large selection of appetizers and desserts are served while an invisible pianist (the ghostly "Annabelle") plays show tunes. The whole audience then moves to the intimate showroom, where they're treated to a wonderful display of sleight-of-hand magic by Warren Gibson, many of whose tricks are truly mind-boggling.

PLACES Lahaina

▼ OLD LAHAINA LŪ'AU

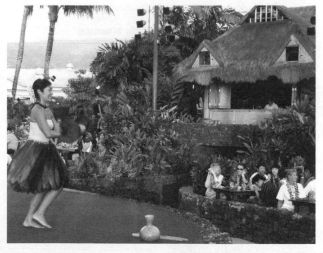

Kā'anapali

Until 1957, there had never been a town at Kā'anapali – just a small plantation wharf served by a short railroad from the sugar mill at Lahaina. What Kā'anapali did have, however, was a superb white-sand beach – far better than anything at Lahaina – backed by a tract of land that was ripe for development and more than twice the size of Waikīkī. Kā'anapali's first hotel opened in 1963, and has been followed by half a dozen similar giants, whose four thousand rooms now welcome half a million visitors each year. There's not much else here, however, but it's a pretty enough place, with its palm-fringed beach, two rolling golf courses, and sunset views of the island of Lanai filling the western horizon.

Kā'anapali Beach

Kā'anapali Beach is divided into two separate long strands by the forbidding, three-hundred-foot cinder cone of Pu'u Keka'a, known as the Black Rock. The sand shelves away abruptly from both sections, so swimmers soon find themselves in deep water, but bathing is usually safe outside periods of high winter surf. The rugged lava coastline around the Black Rock itself, close to the *Sheraton*, is one of the best snorkeling spots on Maui, with an extensive and remarkably tame population of

▼ KĀ'ANAPALI BEACH

colorful fish. As ever in Hawaii, where every beach is publicly owned, you don't have to stay at one of Kā'anapali's hotels to use the main beach. There are also a couple of public beach parks – Hanaka'ō'ō and Wahikuli – just around the headland to the south. Swimming is generally safer at Wahikuli, but the facilities and general ambience are more appealing at Hanaka'ō'ō.

Whale Museum

Daily 9am–10pm. Free. A pavilion at the main (inland) entrance to the Whalers Village mall shelters the articulated skeleton of a sperm whale, whose vestigial "fingers" are visible in its flippers. Nearby, a mock-up of a small nineteenth-century whaleboat is fully labeled with its various esoteric components and gadgets. Both serve by way of introduction to the gripping, if somewhat grisly, Whale Museum, which takes up half the mall's uppermost floor.

This free exhibition is devoted to Maui's former heyday as a

▲ WHALE MUSEUM

whaling center, illustrating the tedium and the terror of the seamen's daily routine through scrimshaw, shellwork valentines, logbooks, tools, letters, and bills. As well as a scale model of the whaling bark *Sunbeam*, there's a large cast-iron "try pot"; though used for reducing whale blubber at sea, they gave rise to the stereotyped but not entirely untrue image of cannibals cooking missionaries in big black cauldrons.

Contrary to what you might imagine, no actual killing of whales took place in Hawaiian waters. Hawaii was simply the place where the whaling ships came to recuperate after hunting much further north in the Pacific. What's more, the humpback – the whale most commonly found in Hawaiian waters – was not hunted at all during the nineteenth century. The target for the fleets was instead the right whale, so named, logically enough, because it was deemed the "right" whale to kill.

Shops

Whalers Village

While even the most inveterate shopper would probably not bother to drive to Kā'anapali just to visit the Whalers Village mall, it does hold a reasonable array of stores, almost all geared towards tourists. Martin & MacArthur is good for Hawaiian crafts and tiki-style souvenirs; there's a Borders Express with several shelves of Hawaii-related books and maps; Lahaina Printsellers stock good maps and prints; Reyn's has well-priced aloha wear; and you'll also find international chains like The Body Shop and Prada. Besides the restaurants listed below, there's a food court on the lower level with Korean, Japanese, and Italian outlets, plus an espresso bar.

Restaurants

Hula Grill

Whalers Village ☎808/667-6636. This large, long oceanfront restaurant, open to the sea breezes and offering great views at lunchtime, features live Hawaiian music nightly. Chef Peter Merriman, who is known for his distinctively Hawaiian take on things, prepares some interesting appetizers, such as a Hawaiian *ceviche* – fish marinated in lime, Maui onion, and coconut milk ($7) – along with plenty of dim sum and sashimi, while the $18–28 entrees include "screamin' sesame" fish and banana barbecue ribs, baked in an *imu*, or underground oven.

Rusty Harpoon

Whalers Village ☎808/661-3123. Daily 8am–midnight. A beachfront

RESTAURANTS	
Hula Grill	3
Rusty Harpoon	3
Swan Court	1
Tiki Terrace	2
Va Bene	4

0   Yards 400

Pu'ukoli'i Station

Kā'anapali Station

Sugar Cane Train

HONOAPI'ILANI HIGHWAY

KAI ALA DRIVE

KEKA'A DRIVE

Whalers Village

Whale Museum

KĀ'ANAPALI PARKWAY

NOHEA KAI DRIVE

ACCOMMODATION

Hyatt Regency Maui	C
Kā'anapali Beach Hotel	D
Maui Eldorado Resort	B
Maui Marriott Resort and Ocean Club	H
Royal Lahaina Resort	A
Sheraton Maui	G
The Westin Maui	F
The Whaler on Kā'anapali Beach	E

Kā'anapali Beach

Pu'u Keka'a (Black Rock)

Kā'anapali / Hanaka'ō'ō Beach

KĀ'ANAPALI

mall restaurant, with terrace and covered seating, the *Rusty Harpoon* has a simple, inexpensive lunch menu with inventive daily specials, such as a seafood curry casserole ($13) and more traditional dinner entrees such as steaks, ribs, and fresh fish ($20–32). A limited "Happy Hour" menu is served 2–6pm and 10pm–midnight, and there's also a $15 set dinner menu 5–6pm only.

Swan Court

Hyatt Regency Maui, 200 Nohea Kai Drive ☏808/661-1234. Sublimely romantic resort restaurant, laid out around a lagoon populated by live swans and flamingos. Breakfast, served daily, is a relaxed joy; for dinner, Tues–Sat only, the food is expensive but exquisite. Appetizers like the crab and lobster cheesecake cost around $16, though you can also get a delicious Thai corn chowder for $8, while entrees at around $40 include a fabulous combo of grilled *opah* (moonfish) and New Zealand mussels, or a distinctly un-Hawaiian pepper-seared bison in a coffee-honey sauce.

▼ SWAN COURT

▲ DRUMS OF THE PACIFIC

Tiki Terrace

Kāʻanapali Beach Hotel, 2525 Kāʻanapali Parkway ☎ 808/667-0124. This unassuming hotel restaurant attempts to serve traditional Hawaiian foods, meaning plenty of fish, plus local ingredients like taro and sweet potato, much of it steamed in ti-leaf parcels. That sounds like a good idea, and the food itself isn't bad; at dinner, when there's cheesy Hawaiian entertainment, entrees cost $18–30. However, the open-air "tiki grill" section makes it a favorite with families with young kids, and as a result it tends to be both hectic and a bit messy.

Va Bene

Maui Marriott, 100 Nohea Kai Drive ☎ 808/667-1200. The *Marriott*'s principal dining room, open for breakfast and dinner daily plus brunch ($27) on Sunday mornings, enjoys a gorgeous oceanfront setting; if you can get an open-air table on the lawns at sunset, you're in for a real treat. Breakfasts are conventional enough, with a healthy buffet ($14.50) and a cholesterol-packed version ($19.50), while dinner focuses on zesty Italian dishes, with a full range of meat and seafood entrees costing $20–28. There's also a prime rib buffet ($29) on Fridays and an Alaskan lobster buffet on Saturdays ($39).

Shows

Drums of the Pacific

Hyatt Regency Maui, Kāʻanapali ☎ 808/661-1234. Daily 5pm. $79, teenagers $52, under-13s $37. If you're looking for the full *lūʻau* experience, you won't get it from the *Hyatt Regency*'s evening show. Though it's set just yards from the sea, guests remain seated at long tables throughout, so you barely even see the sunset. The buffet-style food is pretty good, but the menu is very limited, with just a handful of dishes including *kālua* pork and chunks of beef, and there's little attempt to explain its Hawaiian origins or traditions. The show itself, however, isn't bad, with a full panoply of *hula* dancers and Polynesian performers, climaxing in a display of fire-eating.

Northwest Maui

Heavily developed in stretches with mostly small-scale condos and hotels, the coastline of Northwest Maui is home to idyllic beaches too – though they're not often easily spotted through all the resorts. The climate is significantly wetter just a few miles out of Kā'anapali, and the landscape in turns grows greener, with development petering out altogether beyond upscale Kapalua. The road continues to the legendary surf spot of Honolua Bay, before dwindling to a single lane as the Kahekili Highway. On the map, this looks like a good route to Wailuku, but it's a dangerous drive. What's more, it's certainly not a shortcut; you have to allow well over an hour for the journey. That said, while not quite matching the road to Hāna, the Kahekili Highway is exhilaratingly beautiful, and provides a rare glimpse of how Maui must have looked before the advent of tourism.

Honokōwai, Kahana, and Nāpili

The three communities of Honokōwai, Kahana, and Nāpili that appear on maps just north of Kā'anapali are only nominally distinct; each blends seamlessly into the next, and none holds an ounce of interest for casual visitors. Ignored by the main highway as it heads for Kapalua and beyond, they're linked by Lower Honoapi'ilani Road, which branches down towards the ocean about a mile out of Kā'anapali. To its left stands a succession of all but identical hotels, to its right you'll find the occasional little mall holding one or two stores or restaurants.

Nāpili Bay

This half-mile crescent of perfect if steeply shelving white sand, commanding beautiful views across to Molokai, is filled each day with families staying at adjacent hotels like the *Mauian* (see p.154). The waves that break right on shore can be pretty fierce, and there's often a strong undertow too, but the snorkeling a little further out is excellent,

▲ NĀKĀLELE POINT

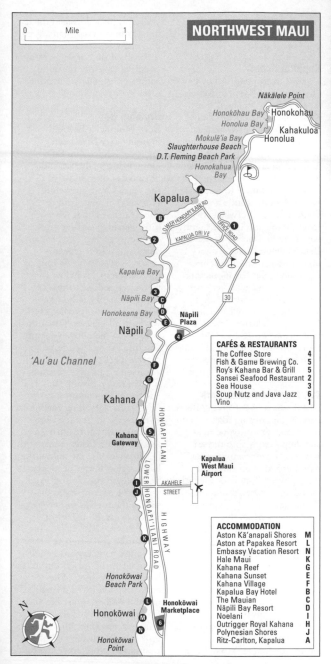

NORTHWEST MAUI

0 Mile 1

Nākālele Point

Honokōhau Bay Honokohau

Honolua Bay

Mokulēʻia Bay Kahakuloa

Slaughterhouse Beach Honolua

D.T. Fleming Beach Park

Honokahua Bay

Kapalua

LOWER HONOAPIʻILANI RD

OFFICE ROAD

KAPALUA DRIVE

Kapalua Bay

Nāpili Bay

Honokeana Bay Nāpili Plaza

Nāpili

ʻAuʻau Channel

HONOAPIʻILANI

Kahana

Kahana Gateway

Kapalua West Maui Airport

LOWER HONOAPIʻILANI HIGHWAY ROAD

AKAHELE STREET

Honokōwai Beach Park

Honokōwai Marketplace

Honokōwai

Honokōwai Point

CAFÉS & RESTAURANTS	
The Coffee Store	4
Fish & Game Brewing Co.	5
Roy's Kahana Bar & Grill	5
Sansei Seafood Restaurant	2
Sea House	3
Soup Nutz and Java Jazz	6
Vino	1

ACCOMMODATION	
Aston Kāʻanapali Shores	M
Aston at Papakea Resort	L
Embassy Vacation Resort	N
Hale Maui	K
Kahana Reef	G
Kahana Sunset	E
Kahana Village	F
Kapalua Bay Hotel	B
The Mauian	C
Nāpili Bay Resort	D
Noelani	I
Outrigger Royal Kahana	H
Polynesian Shores	J
Ritz-Carlton, Kapalua	A

especially in the morning, and there's plenty of shelter from both wind and sun.

Kapalua Beach

Kapalua, at the end of Lower Honoapi'ilani Road in Maui's far northwest corner, is the West Maui equivalent of the exclusive resort of Wailea, at the southwest tip of East Maui. Relatively few tourists stray into this pristine enclave, whose luxurious hotels capitalize well on their proximity to Kapalua Beach. A perfect little arc of white sand, set between two rocky headlands, it is frequently voted the best beach in the US. Besides being pretty, it's also one of Maui's safest beaches, especially good for snorkeling and diving, and even receives occasional visits from monk seals. The one drawback to Kapalua is that the climate is undeniably worse even this short distance north of Lahaina, with rain and cloud more likely to drift in from the northeast.

D.T. Fleming Beach Park

The dunes at D.T. Fleming Beach Park, in Honokahua Bay, are knit together with ironwood trees and drop sharply into the sea. It can be a dangerous spot for swimming, though surfers love the big waves. Full park amenities, including showers, restrooms, picnic tables, and the presence of lifeguards, make this a popular destination for local families.

Slaughterhouse Beach

At several points along the highway beyond Honokahua Bay, the landowners, Maui Pineapple, have built fences to stop people from clambering down through the undergrowth to shaded, sandy Slaughterhouse Beach at Mokulē'ia Bay. Keep

your eyes peeled instead for the top of the concrete stairway that provides safe access; look for cars parked on the verge. Winter conditions usually preclude bathing, but nude sunbathing carries on year-round.

Honolua Bay

Both Mokulē'ia Bay and Honolua Bay have been set aside as a Marine Life Conservation District, and in summer offer some of the island's best snorkeling. Honolua's major claim to fame, however, is as Maui's most heralded surfing spot, and between September and April, the waters regularly swarm with surfers. As long as the swell remains below five feet, intermediate surfers can enjoy some of the longest-lasting and most predictable waves in all Hawaii. When they exceed ten feet, however, only absolute experts can hope to survive; perils include not only a fearsome cave that seems to suck in every passing stray, but cut-throat competition from other surfers. Parking for surfers is at several ad hoc lots along the rough dirt roads that line the pineapple fields covering the headland on the far side of the bay. Large galleries of spectators assemble on the clifftop to watch the action, while the surfers themselves slither down to the ocean by means of treacherous trails.

To reach the beach at Honolua, park instead beside the road at the inland end of the bay and walk down. The access path is the width of a road, but the surface is terrible and driving on it is illegal. Taking it will lead you through a weird, lush forest with the feel of a Louisiana bayou: every tree, and even the barbed-wire fence, has been throttled by creeping vines. Across a (usually dry) streambed lies the neat, rocky curve of the beach itself, with the eastern end of Molokai framed in the mouth of the bay.

Honokōhau Bay

Though only five miles out of Kapalua, Honokōhau Bay feels like another world. The entire valley is swamped by a dense canopy of flowering trees; there's a hidden village in there, but it's hard to spot a single building. The beach itself is a small crescent of gray pebbles, used only by fishermen.

Nākālele Point

The Kahekili Highway begins at Maui's northernmost limit, Nākālele Point, a rolling expanse of grassy heathland that fell victim a few years ago to a bizarre craze that swept most of Hawaii. In remote spots all over the islands, people suddenly started erecting miniature stone cairns, under the impression that they were maintaining an ancient tradition. Stacks of perhaps a dozen small rocks are dotted all over the landscape, and many visitors have also used pebbles to spell out their names or other messages – much to the displeasure of Maui Pineapple, which still owns the land.

Various deeply rutted dirt roads drop away from the highway towards the sea in this area, starting both from the parking lot at milepost 38 and from another more makeshift lot half a mile further on. Hiking in that direction enables you to inspect the small light beacon that warns passing ships of the rocky headland, and an impressive natural blowhole in the oceanfront shelf.

Kahakuloa Head

Beyond Nākālele Point, the Kahekili Highway seems to wind endlessly along the extravagantly indented coastline. Often very narrow, but always smoothly surfaced, it alternates between scrubby exposed promontories, occasionally capable of supporting a pale meadow, and densely green, wet valleys.

A few miles along, the huge and very un-Hawaiian-looking crag of Kahakuloa Head towers 636ft above the eastern entrance to Kahakuloa Bay. The name means "tall lord," on account of its supposed resemblance to a member of the chiefly class, the *ali'i*, wearing a feathered cape; alongside it stands his attendant, a lesser peak known as Pu'u Kāhuli'anapa. The verdant valley that stretches back from both once ranked among the most populous on Maui, and still looks like a classic *ahupua'a* – the fundamental ancient land division, reaching from the sea to the mountain via low-lying taro terraces and groves of palms and fruit trees.

▼ KAHAKULOA HEAD

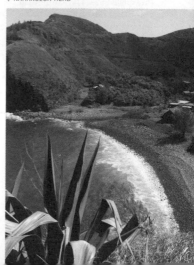

Kahakuloa

The perfect little village of Kahakuloa is poised just behind its beach of black and gray boulders. Close to the green clapboard church as you drive in, a couple of fruit stands, laden with fresh pineapples and other goodies, make tempting places to stop. The streambed is lined with trees, while dirt roads crisscross the valley between the fields and the ramshackle houses. A little further back nestles the simple wooden structures of St Francis Xavier Mission, built in 1846.

Cafés

The Coffee Store

Nāpili Plaza, 5095 Nāpili Hau St, Nāpili ☎808/669-4170, ⊛www.mauicoffee .com. Small espresso bar busy with locals from 6.30am daily, that, as well as pastries and sandwiches, also offers Internet access.

Restaurants

Fish & Game Brewing Company & Rotisserie

Kahana Gateway, 4405 Honoapi'ilani Hwy ☎808/669-3474. Large mall complex consisting of a pub serving pilsners, stouts, and wheat beers brewed on the premises, and an open restaurant area dominated by a *kiawe* grill and an oyster bar. The food is surprisingly good for mall fare, with grilled ribs or chicken for

under $20, a colossal steak for $28, and fresh fish prepared in various styles for around $27. A lighter, limited menu is served during the afternoon and until 1am nightly.

Roy's Kahana Bar & Grill

Kahana Gateway, 4405 Honoapi'ilani Hwy ☎808/669-6999, ⊛www .roysrestaurant.com. Celebrity chef Roy Yamaguchi's Maui showcase is open for dinner only – which is just as well, given its lack of views. The aromas of its superb "Euro-Asian" food waft from its open kitchen as soon as you walk in. Signature dishes such as hibachi salmon, "butterfish" (black cod) steamed with *miso*, and "Roy's 'Original' Blackened Rare *Ahi*" appear on the menu as both appetizers (around $12) and entrees (more like $25); there are also several mouthwatering specials each night.

Sansei Seafood Restaurant

The Shops at Kapalua, 115 Bay Drive, Kapalua ☎808/669-6286. Top-quality, dinner-only seafood specialist, adjoining the *Kapalua Bay Hotel*, which also has an outlet in Kīhei. Both decor and menu are fundamentally Japanese, though there's a strong Pacific Rim element as well. The fresh sushi selection includes a mouthwatering mango crab salad roll ($8), while seared salmon and seafood pasta ($20), and daily fish specials ($25), are among the entrees. Certain items, like the $5 crispy fried *onaga* (snapper) head and the Korean spiced raw octopus, are playfully labeled "for locals only." There's also karaoke until 1am on Thursday and Friday nights.

Sea House

Nāpili Kai Beach Resort, 5500 Lower Honoapi'ilani Rd, Nāpili ☎808/669-1500.

▼ VINO

Very popular seafront restaurant, right on Nāpili Beach at the most expensive of the oceanside condo resorts. The food is good without being exceptional – conventional American breakfasts for under $10; lunchtime soups, salads, sandwiches, or sushi rolls for $9 12; and

▲ MASTERS OF HAWAIIAN SLACK KEY GUITAR

steak or seafood dinners for more like $30 – but the views, from the oceanside tables at least, are great. Every Tuesday at 5.30pm, local kids put on a display of *hula* and Hawaiian culture, for $50 including dinner.

Soup Nutz and Java Jazz

Honokōwai Marketplace, 3350 Lower Honoapi'ilani Rd ☎808/667-0787, ⓦwww.javajazz.net. Funky juice and espresso bar, with lots of comfy seating and a steady jazz soundtrack. The menu includes breakfast eggs and omelets ($8–11), smoothies ($4), falafel and other lunchtime sandwiches (under $10); and evening specials range up to steak and lobster ($18–28). Mon–Sat 6am–9pm, Sun 6am–5pm.

Vino

Kapalua Village Golf Course Clubhouse, Kapalua ☎808/661-8466. Though this surprising but superb restaurant, just off the main highway above the Kapalua resorts, is the brainchild of the Japanese chef/owner of *Sansei*, here the specialty is Italian, not sushi. Or rather, Italian with a definite Hawaiian tinge, with ingredients like Kona lobster and raw *ahi* alongside the pasta and gnocchi dishes. Two further characteristics distinguish the menu: a large selection of *tapas*-sized portions,

most costing $7–10, which enable you to sample several very disparate dishes, and the particular attention afforded to wine, with special pairings devised for most dishes. If you prefer a more conventional meal, a "large plate" – a full-sized entree, such as *osso bucco* or horseradish-crusted short rib – costs $19–25.

Shows

Masters of Hawaiian Slack Key Guitar

Ritz-Carlton, Kapalua, 1 Ritz-Carlton Drive, Kapalua ☎808/669-3858 or 1-888/669-3858, ⓦwww.slackkey .com. Mid-Dec to mid-Sept Tues 6pm & 8.30pm, mid-Sept to mid-Dec Tues 7.30pm. $35, Hawaii residents $25. The *Ritz-Carlton's* ongoing series of slack key guitar concerts is an absolute treat. The fact that it presents traditional Hawaiian music in a slightly dreary conference-room setting doesn't stop the evenings from being gloriously happy events, thanks largely to virtuoso emcee George Kahumoku, Jr. Each week sees a different guest star, from the very biggest names of the genre – regulars include Cyril Pahinui, Led Kaapana, Carlos Andrade, and Auntie Genoa Keawe.

Kahului

Although Kahului is the largest town on Maui – it holds the island's principal harbor and airport, and most of its major shopping centers – it's not an interesting, let alone historic, place to visit. A couple of inexpensive hotels stake a claim for Kahului as a central base, but there's next to nothing to see here, and you could miss it altogether with a clear conscience. Still, you'll probably find yourself calling in repeatedly, to buy supplies, grab a snack as you race round the island, or perhaps shop at the comprehensive Queen Ka'ahumanu Center and attend a show at the prestigious Maui Arts and Cultural Center.

Maui Arts and Cultural Center

1 Cameron Way, Kahului Beach Rd, Kahului ☏808/242-ARTS, box office ☏808/242-7469, ⓦwww.mauiarts .org. Just off the busy Kahului Beach Road, which curves around Kahului Harbor, the Maui Arts and Cultural Center is Maui's premier venue for the visual and performing arts. In

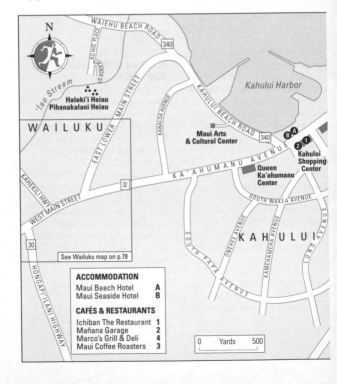

ACCOMMODATION

Maui Beach Hotel — A
Maui Seaside Hotel — B

CAFÉS & RESTAURANTS

Ichiban The Restaurant — 1
Mañana Garage — 2
Marco's Grill & Deli — 4
Maui Coffee Roasters — 3

See Wailuku map on p.78

Maui's main port

Having started the nineteenth century as a small cluster of grass shacks, Kahului grew in tandem with the expansion of commercial agriculture. After the Kahului and Wailuku Railroad opened in 1879, it channeled the sugar and pineapple crops of central Maui down to the wharves of Kahului. At first Kahului was an unsanitary place: a major outbreak of plague in 1900 forced the authorities to burn down the oceanfront Chinatown district and ring the whole town with rat-proof fences. When it was rebuilt, the harbor was greatly expanded and dredged to provide the only deep-water anchorage on the island. Kahului thereafter supplanted Lahaina as Maui's main port and has remained so to this day, welcoming cruise ships whose passengers are instantly whisked away to more scenic parts of the island.

addition to a four-thousand-seat open-air amphitheater, it houses two separate indoor theaters and an art gallery that hosts changing temporary exhibitions. Those big-name musicians who make it as far as Maui – more than you might expect, as it's a favorite final stop for trans-America touring bands – play here, while the Maui Symphony Orchestra (☎808/244-5439) puts on half a dozen concerts each winter.

In addition, the center's Castle Theater operates as a movie theater in conjunction with the

Maui Film Festival (☎808/572-3456, ◉www.mauifilmfestival.com). The festival itself takes place in Wailea each June, but every Wednesday evening the Castle Theater shows a current release, and each December it also puts on nightly "Academy Screenings" of potential Oscar contenders.

Kanahā Pond State Wildlife Sanctuary

Half a mile west of Kahului Airport, just before Hwy-36A meets Hwy-36. A tiny roadside parking lot marks the only public access to this marshy saltwater lagoon. Used as a fishpond until it was choked by the mud dredged up from Kahului Harbor, the sanctuary is now set aside for the protection of endangered bird species, among them the black-necked *ae'o* stilt and the *'auku'u* (night heron).

There are no official opening hours; visitors simply make their way through the gate and follow a pedestrian causeway for fifty yards out to a windy, open-sided viewing shelter. Although it's not a very prepossessing spot, with the factories of Kahului Harbor clearly visible off to the left, and planes passing low overhead as they descend into the airport, it's surprisingly peaceful, and waterfowl do indeed seem to like it. Wading birds can almost

always be spotted picking their way through the shallow waters, though when it comes to smaller species you're likely to hear more than you actually see.

Kanahā Beach County Park

Alahao Street. Kahului's most popular oceanfront spot, despite its proximity to the airport runways, is the large Kanahā Beach County Park. In the daytime at least, aircraft noise barely impacts on beachgoers, while the shallow, choppy turquoise waters are ideal for novice windsurfers, who come from all over the world to swirl back and forth against the backdrop of 'Īao Valley and the West Maui Mountains. Among companies offering windsurfing lessons here (at around $79 for 2hr 30min, including equipment rental) are Action Sports Maui (☎808/871-5857, ◉www.actionsportsmaui.com) and Alan Cadiz's HST Windsurfing School (☎808/871-5423 or 1-800/968-5423, ◉www.hstwindsurfing.com).

Windsurfers ready for the big time graduate to Ho'okipa, just a few miles east but light-years away in terms of difficulty.

For its full length, the beach is fringed by pine trees, with countless shoots sprouting from the dunes, and fallen needles creating a soft carpet just behind. The lawns under the trees have picnic tables, though to buy food or drink you have to drive back into Kahului.

There is a campground here, administered by the county parks office (see p.160), with seven individual sites ($3 per night) limited to a maximum three-night stay, but the nearness of the airport and busy town makes it hard to recommend.

▼ KAHANĀ BEACH

▲ ALEXANDER & BALDWIN SUGAR MUSEUM

Alexander & Baldwin Sugar Museum

3957 Hansen Rd at Hwy-350, Puʻunēnē ☏808/871-8058, ⓦwww .sugarmuseum.com. Mon–Sat 9.30am–4.30pm. $5, under-18s $2.
There's no missing the rusty red hulk of the Puʻunēnē Sugar Mill, which forces Hwy-350 to make a sharp right turn a mile south of Kahului. Still belching smoke as it consumes the cane from the surrounding fields, this was the largest sugar mill in the world when it was built in 1902, and now stands as one of only two such mills still operational in Hawaii – the other is on Kauai.

Easily overlooked, however, is the smaller building just across from the mill, which houses the Alexander & Baldwin Sugar Museum. The museum relates the history of sugar production on Maui, a tale of nineteenth-century scheming and skullduggery that, well over a century later, may not be capable of holding your interest for very long.

Scale models include a whirring but incomprehensible re-creation of the main mill machinery, and a relief map of the whole island. More illuminating displays focus on the lives of the plantation laborers, showing the thick clothes they wore to protect against the dust and poisonous centipedes, and the numbered bango tags by which they were identified in place of names. No bones are made of the fact that the multi-ethnic workforce was deliberately, but ultimately unsuccessfully, segregated to avoid solidarity. The museum store is well stocked with books on ethnic and labor history, as well as souvenir packets of raw sugar.

Shops

Queen Kaʻahumanu Center

275 Kaʻahumanu Ave, Kahului ☏808/877-3369. Kahului's smartest and largest shopping mall, the Queen Kaʻahumanu Center is anchored by Macy's and Sears department stores, as well as their more distinctive Japanese counterpart Tamakawaya – which has a good, cheap deli counter. It also holds a fair assortment of specialty stores, including the arts and crafts specialists Maui Hands, and the surf and beach wear of Local Motion. Various

▼ QUEEN KAʻAHUMANU CENTER

upscale restaurants and bars have tried to establish themselves here only to falter within a year or two, but there is a reasonable open-air food court upstairs.

Maui Marketplace

Dairy Road at Hukilike Street. Away from central Kahului, the Maui Marketplace mall is noteworthy as the home of the island's best bookstore – a giant Borders (Mon–Thurs 9am–11pm, Fri & Sat 9am–midnight, Sun 9am–10pm; ☎808/877-6160).

▲ ICHIBAN

Cafés

Maui Coffee Roasters

444 Hāna Hwy ☎808/877-2877. This relaxed, daytime-only espresso bar with hand-painted tables is a popular hangout for windsurfers from the nearby beaches. Vegetarian wraps and sandwiches, like focaccia with mozzarella, are $6–8; try the fabulous raspberry-and-white-chocolate scones.

Restaurants

Ichiban The Restaurant

Kahului Shopping Center, 47 Ka'ahumanu Ave ☎808/871-6977. Closed Sun. Large mall eatery, which serves American and continental breakfasts, then devotes itself for the remainder of the day to Japanese cuisine. For lunch there's *saimin* for $5, *donburi* bowls for $6, and teriyakis for $6–8; at dinner you can get shrimp or chicken stir-fries, *udon* noodles, and sushi rolls for under $10.

Mañana Garage

33 Lono Ave ☎808/873-0220. Closed Sat. This Latin American–Mexican restaurant, kitted out with a cheery, vaguely post-industrial decor and located in an office building right on Ka'ahumanu Avenue, serves a creative but somewhat overpriced menu ranging from fish tacos to guava salmon to paella. It's popular with locals for lunch, and, thanks to a viewless but spacious terrace, for after-work drinks. Typical entrees cost around $12 for lunch, up to $30 in the evening. Live music and dancing most nights.

Marco's Grill & Deli

395 Dairy Rd ☎808/877-4446. Lively Italian restaurant, in a modern mall not far from the airport. Once the breakfast omelets, pancakes, and espressos have finished, the lunch and dinner menus feature deli sandwiches, pizzas (from $11), and rich meat and seafood pastas, including rigatoni with prosciutto in a vodka sauce ($18).

Wailuku

Located at the mouth of the fertile and spectacular ʻĪao Valley and within a few miles of the lush valleys that line the windward coast of West Maui, Wailuku has a very different geography to, and a much more venerable history than, its close neighbor to the east, Kahului. This was what might be called the *poi* bowl of Maui, at the heart of the largest taro-growing area in Hawaii, and was home to generations of priests and warriors in ancient times. These days Wailuku is a sleepy sort of place, easily seen in less than half a day. Nonetheless, it's one of the few towns on Maui that still feels like a genuine community, and can serve as a welcome antidote to the sanitized charms of the modern resorts elsewhere.

PLACES Wailuku

Downtown Wailuku

The heart of Wailuku is where Main Street, the continuation of Kaʻahumanu Avenue, crosses Market Street. Both streets hold a small assortment of shops, the most interesting of which are the faded antique and junk stores along Market Street to the north, just before it drops down to cross the ʻĪao Stream. Also look for the 1929 ʻĪao Theater, an attractive little playhouse on Market Street that typically puts on six Broadway-type shows each year (season runs Sept–June; ☎808/242-6969, ⊛www.mauionstage.com).

Kaʻahumanu Church, at the intersection of Main and High streets, was founded in 1832. Naming it after Queen Kaʻahumanu, a convert to Christianity who was largely responsible for the destruction of the old Hawaiian

religion (see p.132), was the idea of the Queen herself. The current building, whose four-story white spire has a clock face on each side, dates from 1876. It's not usually open to visitors, but you're welcome to attend the Hawaiian-language services at 9am on Sunday mornings.

The Bailey House

2375-A Main St ☎808/244-3326, ⊛www.mauimuseum.org. Mon–Sat 10am–4pm. $5, ages 7–13 $1, under-7 free. The island's oldest house and the best museum of general

▼ DOWNTOWN WAILUKU

history on the island, the Bailey
House sits on what was once
Maui's most highly prized plot
of land. A royal compound
here formerly controlled access
to the sacred 'Īao Valley. Local
chiefs donated it during the
1830s so the Central Maui
Mission could build day schools
to teach both adults and
children to read. From 1837
until 1849, it was also the site of
the Wailuku Female Seminary,
a boarding school designed to
produce "good Christian wives"
for the male graduates of the
Lahainaluna Seminary.

The first occupant of the
house was Reverend Jonathan
Green, who resigned from the
mission in 1842 to protest the
fact that the American Board
of Commissioners for Foreign
Missions accepted money from
slave-owners. For the next fifty
years, it was home to Edward
Bailey and his wife Caroline
Hubbard Bailey. He was a
minister, schoolmaster, carpenter,
and amateur painter, while she is

remembered in the name of the
long "Mother Hubbard" dresses,
also known as *mu'umu'us*, that
she made for local women.

After an entertaining
introductory talk, visitors can
wander through rooms filled
with period furniture, none
of which originally belonged
here. The largest room
focuses on ancient Hawaiian
history, with archeological
finds from Maui, Lanai, and
Kahoolawe, including bones,
clubs, shark's-tooth weapons,
and *leis* of shells and feathers.
One large wooden platter was
used for serving boiled dog
– a popular dish for native
Hawaiian women, who were
forbidden to eat pork. There's
also a copy of the only carved
temple image ever found on
Maui, a likeness of the pig-god
Kamapua'a that was discovered
in a remote Upcountry cave.
Both the Baileys and the
ancient Hawaiians alike would
be appalled to see such a sacred
item on public display. On the

wall there's a portrait of the unruly chief Boki, who sailed to the South Seas in 1829 in search of sandalwood to replace Hawaii's vanished crop and died in an explosion at sea.

A gallery downstairs holds local landscapes painted by the white-bearded Edward Bailey in his old age, while the upstairs rooms are preserved more or less as the Baileys would have known them, with a quilt of the Hawaiian flag spread across the four-poster bed.

Haleki'i and Pihanakalani heiaus

Follow Hwy-333 out of Wailuku to the north, double back south along Waiehu Beach Road, turn inland at Kuhio Place, and take the first left, Hea Place. Daily 7am–7pm. Free.

The twin ancient temples of Haleki'i and Pihanakalani guard the Wailuku Plain from two separate hillocks near the mouth of the 'Iao Stream. With rows of low-budget housing to the north, and the industrial area of Kahului to the south, this is not the most evocative of sites, but raising your gaze towards the horizon provides fine views of the ocean and the turquoise waters of the harbor and, in the early morning, mighty Haleakalā can often be seen in its entirety. The short trail from the parking lot leads through scrubby soil – these hillocks are, in fact, lithified sand dunes – to Haleki'i Heiau. Maui's ruling chief, Kahekili, lived at this "house of images" during religious ceremonies in the 1760s, when its uppermost platform would have held thatched huts interspersed with carved effigies of the gods. The hilltop is now bare, and the only remnants of the *heiau* are the lower stone terraces dropping down the side towards Kahului.

Both Haleki'i and Pihanakalani *heiaus* were *luakinis*, or temples dedicated to the war god Ku that were the site of human sacrifices. Pihanakalani seems to have been originally constructed sometime between 1260 and 1400 AD, and reoriented to face towards the Big Island during the eighteenth century, which archeologists see as a sign that the chiefs of Maui must have been preparing an attack. When Kamehameha the Great's Big Island warriors finally conquered Maui in 1790, they celebrated their victory at 'Iao Valley with a rededication ceremony at Pihanakalani that included its final human sacrifice. Like all ancient Hawaiian temples, it was stripped of its images and largely dismantled after the death of Kamehameha, which coincided with the arrival of the first Christian missionaries. Significantly more traces survive than of Haleki'i, however, so it's worth continuing this far, by following the main path to the far side of the gulch and then turning left.

▼ THE BAILEY HOUSE

Waihe'e Valley Trail

Five miles north of Wailuku. While
the best-known of the many
valleys that pierce the West
Maui Mountains is 'Iao Valley,
the only one that you can
penetrate to any extent on foot
is Waihe'e Valley. In recent years,
much to the dismay of local
residents, increasing numbers of
tourists have become aware that
the Waihe'e Valley Trail offers
the only chance to experience
the rainforest on this side of
the island, with the bonus of
close-up waterfall views. Fierce
disputes over public access to
the valley have now finally been
resolved, however, with the
solution that it's open for set
hours only, and an admission
fee is payable (daily 9am–5pm;
adults $5, ages 5–10 $2). Only
consider coming on fine days;
if rain is at all likely, there's a
serious risk of flash floods.

To reach the trail, turn *mauka*
(inland) from the Kahekili
Highway onto Waihe'e Valley
Road, and then turn right half
a mile up, following a dirt road
that ends at a ticket booth-cum-
fruit stand and parking lot. The
trail itself starts out as a dirt
road for its first three quarters
of a mile, which then grows
steadily narrower as it makes
its way deeper into the valley.
After following an irrigation
channel used by local farmers,
which occasionally tunnels
through rock walls although
the path never has to, it reaches
the Waihe'e River, which you
have to cross twice in quick
succession via two long, swaying
suspension footbridges. They're
great fun, though as each is the
width of a single plank (with
cable handrails) they're totally
unsuitable for young children.
Further crossings are required as
you continue, but from here on
they involve wading or hopping
from rock to rock. Assuming
conditions are dry enough for
you to make it all the way, the
trail ends at a scenic shallow
dam, a total of two miles up
from the start. Immediately
below the dam, just across the
river, the 'Ali'ele Falls splash
down from a side valley, while
the highest peaks of the West
Maui Mountains tower further
inland, cleft at one point by the
tall Mananole Falls. Allow two
hours for the round-trip hike.

Waihe'e Ridge Trail

One of Maui's most enjoyable
hikes, the Waihe'e Ridge Trail,

▲ WAIHE'E VALLEY TRAIL

starts a mile up a spur road that branches *mauka* (inland) from Kahekili Highway at milepost 7, opposite the Mendes Ranch three miles north of the village school in Waihe'e. If you get here by driving the Kahekili Highway around West Maui from Kapalua you'll find the turning, which is signposted to *Camp Maluhia*, roughly seven miles south of Kahakuloa. This gorgeous climb, best done in the morning before the clouds set in, takes you as high into the West Maui Mountains as it's possible to go; allow at least two hours, and preferably three, for the round trip.

From the easily spotted parking lot where the road makes a sharp curve right towards the camp itself, the trail starts off as a very clear cement path beyond a barred gate. This is its steepest section, but it soon comes to an end, when you turn left to find yourself in a pine and eucalyptus forest. Before long you emerge from that in turn, to enjoy views down into Waihe'e Valley, over to a double waterfall embedded in the next ridge to the north, and back across the isthmus to Haleakalā Highway snaking up the volcano.

For all this first stretch of the trail, which totals 1.5 miles, it looks as though you're heading for the crest of the ridge ahead. Ultimately, however, the path sidesteps across a brief razorback to reach an unexpected high mountain valley. The terrain here is extremely marshy, but you're soon climbing again, this time through tree-less uplands that feature a much greater preponderance of native Hawaiian plants and shrubs, including some spectacular orchids and also stunted

▲ WAIHE'E RIDGE TRAIL

red- and orange-blossomed *lehua* trees.

The trail ends at an unsheltered picnic table in a clearing 2.25 miles up. The chances are that by now you're well above the cloud line. If you're lucky enough to be here on a clear morning, however, you can see most of northern Maui from this spot, which is the summit of Lanilili ("Small Heaven") Peak but still well short of the overall summit of West Maui. Towering cliffs and waterfalls lie ahead, while, as you look north towards the ocean, the island of Molokai is clearly visible beyond the rocky pinnacle of Kahakuloa.

Shops

Sig Zane Designs
53 Market St ☎ 808/249-8997. Sig Zane is a Big Island textile designer renowned for the elegant simplicity of his fabrics, each of which is strongly rooted in the lore of native Hawaiian plants. As well as the classiest aloha wear to be found in Hawaii, his shop also sells bedding, slippers, and other household goods.

Cafés

Café Marc Aurel
28 N Market St ☎808/244-0852. Closed Sun. Smart and very popular sidewalk café, serving espressos, smoothies, and pastries, and also offering Internet access.

▲ A SAIGON CAFE

Maui Bake Shop & Deli
2092 Vineyard St ☎808/244-7117. Closed Sun & Mon. Patisserie serving healthy deli breakfasts and lunches, with a wide assortment of soups, salads, and quiches as well as wonderful fresh-baked breads, including focaccias, calzones, whole-grain loaves, and sweet brioches. You can eat well for $5 or less.

Restaurants

AK's Cafe
1237 L Market St ☎808/244-8774, ⓦwww.akscafe.com. Closed Sat & Sun. This bright, clean, and highly recommended little restaurant, well away from downtown on the road up from Kahului Harbor, has a mission to improve the health of local residents, with an emphasis on steaming or grilling rather than frying. Great-value lunch specials at $7–8, such as the succulent baked *ono*, and $12–15 dinner entrees like crab cakes, seared *ahi*, or lemongrass duck breast, come with two sides, such as taro or *ulu* (breadfruit).

Kozo Sushi
52 N Market St ☎808/243-5696. Closed Sun. Spotless, central sushi place that mainly provides take-out for local office workers, but also has a couple of tables where you can relish tasty individual rolls ($2 or less), a *nigiri* lunch box ($6.50), or Hawaii's very own spam *musubi* – spam, seaweed, and rice ($1.30).

Saeng's
2119 Vineyard St ☎808/244-1567. Pleasant Thai restaurant, serving high-quality food at bargain prices. Plate lunches, on weekdays only, include honey-lemon chicken and garlic shrimp for $6–8, while selections from the full dinner menu cost a few dollars more.

A Saigon Cafe
1792 Main St ☎808/243-9560. Predominantly Vietnamese restaurant with an extremely wide-ranging and unusual menu, most of it very tasty. Hot and cold noodle dishes and soups, a lot of curries, and seafood stew – even a "Vietnamese *bouillabaisse*" – plus simpler stir-fried and steamed fish specials, and plenty of vegetarian options. A filling noodle dish costs under $10, though some entrees range over $20, while appetizers like summer rolls and "Vietnamese burritos" are around $5.

Central Maui

Measuring just seven miles north to south, the verdant, narrow plains of central Maui, overshadowed by mighty Haleakalā to the east and the West Maui Mountains to the west, are the island's economic heartland. Beyond the stunning 'Īao Valley, however, where ancient chiefs once ruled from a royal enclosure watered by four rivers that flowed down from the West Maui Mountains, the rest of the isthmus was once a dry and relatively barren expanse. Only since sugar barons created irrigation channels to carry water from the eastern flanks of Haleakalā has the land been capable of supporting the agriculture that now makes it so green. In the northeast, the former sugar town of Pā'ia makes an attractive stop-off, offering good dining and shopping, while Mā'alaea in the southwest holds the popular Maui Ocean Center aquarium.

Tropical Gardens of Maui

'Īao Valley Road. Daily 9am–5pm. Free. Spread away below and to the right of 'Īao Valley Road less than a mile west of Wailuku (see Chapter 5), the small, commercial Tropical Gardens of Maui display and sell a colorful assortment of tropical plants from all over the world

▲ KEPANIWAI COUNTY PARK

and mails specimens to the
continental US. It also holds a
small snack bar.

Kepaniwai County Park

ʻĪao Valley Road Daily dawn–dusk. Free.
An attractive public garden set
amid dramatic, curtain-like folds
in the mountains, Kepaniwai
County Park's lawns and
flowerbeds are laid out in themed
areas that pay tribute to Maui's
Japanese, Chinese, and Portuguese
immigrants, among others.
Wandering the serene grounds
you'll come upon a traditional
thatched *hale*, ornamental
pavilions and miniature pagodas,
as well as statues of anonymous
sugar-cane workers and even
Doctor Sun Yat Sen.

Hawaii Nature Center

ʻĪao Valley Road ☏ 808/244-6500,
ⓦ www.hawaiinaturecenter.org.
Daily 10am–4pm. $6, ages 8–12 $4.
Largely an educational facility
for schoolchildren, the Hawaii
Nature Center, immediately
adjoining Kepaniwai County
Park, holds simple exhibitions
on Hawaiian flora, fauna,
and handicrafts. In addition,
however, staff members conduct

recommended guided hikes in
the ʻĪao Valley area (daily 1.30pm;
adults $25, ages 8–12 $23). As
the high-mountain trails are
otherwise closed to visitors, these
provide the only access into the
spectacularly lush wilderness that
lies beyond the Needle. The cost
of the hikes includes admission to
the center and a souvenir T-shirt.

ʻĪao Valley State Park

Daily 7am–7pm. Free. ʻĪao Valley
Road meanders to a dead end
three miles west of Wailuku,
at the parking lot for ʻĪao Valley
State Park, which in all truth
is more of a viewpoint than a
park in its own right. Straight
ahead, you're confronted by the
spectacle of the ʻĪao Needle, a
1200-foot pinnacle of green-clad
lava that's one of Hawaii's most
famous natural spectacles. A short
but steep footpath crosses ʻĪao
Stream and climbs up a nearby
knoll for even better views from
a covered rain shelter.

Despite appearances, the velvety
Needle is not freestanding, but
simply a raised knob at the end
of a sinuous ridge. Towering,
head usually in the clouds, at
the intersection of two lush
valleys, it's what geologists call an
"erosional residual" – a nugget
of hard volcanic rock left behind
when the softer surrounding
rocks were eroded away. The
ancient Hawaiians, with their
usual scatological gusto, named
it Kukaʻemoku, which politely
translates as "broken excreta."

This whole area owes its
existence to the phenomenal
amount of rain that falls on West
Maui; the 5788-foot peak of
Puʻu Kukui, just over two miles
from here, receives more than
four hundred inches per year.
Unless you come early in the
morning, it's likely to be raining
in ʻĪao Valley, but even when it's

The Battle of ʻĪao Valley

For ancient Hawaiians, the gorgeous ʻĪao Valley was the equivalent of Egypt's Valley of the Kings: they buried their royal dead in the long-lost Olopio cave, and access was barred to commoners. In 1790 the valley also came to be the final resting place for Maui warriors defeated by Kamehameha the Great, from the Big Island, in one of the many battles through which he eventually conquered the entire archipelago. Driven back from the shoreline by Kamehameha's fleet of war canoes, the local armies retreated into the valley, where they were bombarded with impunity by the great cannon Lopaka, directed by John Young and Isaac Davis (see p.55). While the defeated general, Kalanikupule, the son of Maui's chief Kahekili, fled across the mountains, the corpses of his men choked ʻĪao Stream. Hence the name by which the battle became known – Kepaniwai, "the water dam."

▲ ʻĪAO VALLEY STATE PARK

pouring you can usually look straight back down the valley to see the dry, sunlit plains of the isthmus. Following a series of accidents, the trails that lead beyond ʻĪao Needle are closed to casual visitors, and can only be explored on the guided hikes run by the Hawaii Nature Center. Climbing the Needle itself is a physical impossibility, owing to the crumbly nature of the rock.

However, two very short paved, but potentially slippery, trails loop down to ʻĪao Stream from the main footpath, one on either side of the stream. Gardens laid out with native plants line the one closer to the parking lot, and the small waterlogged *loʻi* or taro patch here, similar to a paddy

field, offers one of the best angles for photographs, as you look up past the footbridge towards the Needle.

Maui Tropical Plantation

1670 Honoapiʻilani Hwy, Waikapu ☎808/244-7643, ✆www.mauitropicalplantation.com. Daily 9am–5pm. Free. Tram tours daily 10am–4pm, every 45min; $9.50, ages 3–12 $3.50. Though the Maui Tropical Plantation is a principal stop on round-island bus tours, it's ultimately of minimal interest. Visitors are free to walk into the main "Marketplace," where the stalls are piled with plants, fruits, and souvenirs, and then pass into the lackluster gardens beyond to explore pavilions describing the cultivation of macadamia nuts, sugar, coffee, and other local crops. You can see a few more unusual plants on forty-minute tram tours, which take in the spectacular orchids in the nursery before you leave. The indoor *Tropical Restaurant* serves unremarkable buffet lunches between 11am and 2pm (expect long lines), and sandwiches and salads the rest of the day.

Māʻalaea

At the point where Hwy-30 reaches the south coast,

▲ MĀ'ALAEA BAY

Mā'alaea, a former commercial port, has been given a new lease of life as the preferred marina of Maui's cruise and pleasure boats. The largest contingent are the Molokini snorkel boats (see p.170), which collectively bring Mā'alaea to life very early in the morning, when the day's passengers assemble. This is also an ideal time to catch great views of Haleakalā, whose summit pokes out above the ring of clouds that usually obscures it from Kīhei.

Swimming anywhere near Mā'alaea is not recommended, but there are good surfing breaks just to the south, while windsurfers hurtle out into Mā'alaea Bay from the thin and unexciting strip of sand that stretches all the way east to Kīhei.

Maui Ocean Center

192 Mā'alaea Rd, Mā'alaea ☎808/270-7000, ⊛www.mauioceancenter.com. Daily 9am–5pm. $21, ages 3–12 $14. While Mā'alaea is not a town in any meaningful sense, it has acquired a center of sorts,

in the form of the Mā'alaea Harbor Village mall. That in turn focuses on the Maui Ocean Center, a state-of-the-art aquarium providing a colorful introduction to the marine life of Hawaii. It's not quite as large as you might expect from the size of the entrance fee, but its exhibits are well chosen and very well displayed.

The most spectacular section comes first. The coral groves of the Living Reef (some of them fluorescent) hold such species as camouflaged scorpionfish, seahorses, octopuses, and bizarre "upside-down jellyfish." Eerie garden eels poke like blades of grass from the sandy seabed, but the star, of course, is the little *humuhumunukunu kunukuapua'a* – literally, "the triggerfish with a snout like a pig."

Open-air terraces perched above the harbor hold tanks of huge rays and green sea turtles; as a rule, each turtle is kept at the aquarium for just a few months before being fitted with a tracking device and released into the ocean. Further on, additional displays cover the life cycle of whales, and the relationship between Hawaiians and the Sea, illustrating traditional fishing techniques and equipment. A final huge tank holds pelagic, or open-ocean, sea creatures; its walk-through glass tunnel means that you can stand beneath mighty sharks and rays as they swim above your head.

Certified scuba divers can arrange to take an accompanied

The Lahaina Pali Trail

For an account of the Lahaina Pali Trail, which sets off across the southern tip of West Maui from just north of Mā'alaea, see p.56.

dive into the tank for a one-on-one shark encounter (Mon, Wed & Fri 8.30am; $199); some divers have even got married in there.

Kealia Pond National Wildlife Refuge

Māʻalaea Bay ☎808/875-1582. Free. Set back from Māʻalaea Bay and, for most of its length, Hwy-31, brackish Kealia Pond provides a haven for Hawaiian waterbirds as well as migratory species. Seldom more than two feet deep, and varying seasonally in size between around four hundred acres in winter and two hundred in summer, it's a rare enough remnant of Hawaiian wetlands that it's reserved as a wildlife refuge. Long boardwalks reach out across the water, enabling visitors to watch birds like the *aeʻo* or Hawaiian stilt, and the native Hawaiian duck, *koloa maoli*.

Pāʻia

The friendly, laid-back town of Pāʻia is divided into two distinct

sections, both of which began life serving the sugar plantations in the 1870s. Upper Pāʻia, concentrated around the sugar mill half a mile inland, was built on plantation land and held the camps that housed the laborers, as well as company stores and other facilities. Meanwhile, freebooting entrepreneurs set up shop in Lower Pāʻia, at sea level, operating stores, theaters, restaurants, and anything else that might persuade their captive clientele to part with a few pennies.

Both parts of Pāʻia declined apace with the collapse of agriculture, especially after the post–World War II drift to Kahului. The name "Pāʻia" today refers almost exclusively to what used to be Lower Pāʻia, which has re-emerged in recent years as a center for windsurfers and beach bums. The paint-peeling wooden buildings around the bottom end of Baldwin Avenue give it a very similar feel to Makawao, at the top of the road,

▼ MAUI OCEAN CENTER

while its role as the gateway to the Hāna Highway, covered in Chapter 11, keeps its gift stores and galleries busy with browsing tourists.

H.A. Baldwin Beach County Park

A mile west of Pā'ia. Named after Harry Baldwin, son of Henry Baldwin of Alexander & Baldwin fame (see p.75), this was once the official sugar-company beach, and the chimneys of the sugar mill, which closed down in 2000, remain visible for the moment a few hundred yards off the highway, across the still-active cane fields. Popular with locals, the beach itself is reached by a short approach road lined by a graceful curve of palm trees. Perfect bodysurfing waves crash onto its long unprotected stretch of sand, with safer swimming areas at either end.

Shops

Alice in Hulaland

19 Baldwin Ave, Pā'ia ☎808/579-9922. By far the best store on Maui for *tiki*-themed gifts and novelties, Alice in Hulaland is the place to go to pick up all those souvenirs that you'll otherwise kick yourself for not buying, from ceramic *hula* maidens to highball glasses.

Nā Kani O Hula

110 Hāna Hwy at Baldwin Ave, Pā'ia ☎808/573-6332, ⊛www.nakaniohula .com. Exceptional and unusual store-cum-crafts-studio where Gayle Miyaguchi and Kent Apo make and sell authentic *hula* instruments and accessories, including *'ulī 'ulī* gourd rattles decorated with colorful feathers, as well as woven *lau hala* mats, hats, and bags.

Cafés

Anthony's Coffee Co

90C Hāna Hwy, Pā'ia ☎808/579-8340. Small, early-opening coffee bar just west of central Pā'ia, fitted with a churning coffee roaster and serving espressos, pastries, soups, bagels, and deli sandwiches at a handful of indoor tables, plus a wide range of ice creams to go.

▼ NĀ KANI O HULA

▲ MĀ'ALAEA GRILL

PLACES Central Maui

Cakewalk Pā'ia Bakery

Hāna Hwy at Baldwin Ave, Pā'ia ☎808/579-8770. Though this friendly little café does offer one table, its main business lies in selling delicious fresh goodies to Hāna-bound day-trippers. The cookies, cheesecakes, and scones are gorgeous; the deli sandwiches ($6.50) – such as tomato, mozzarella, and basil – are excellent; and a full picnic lunch, including chips and soda, costs $9.

Restaurants

Cafe Mambo

30 Baldwin Ave, Pā'ia ☎808/579-8021. Pale orange diner, just off the highway, serving espressos plus $6–8 burger or sandwich lunches and $13 dinner-time fajita specials. Picnics to go cost from $9 per person, $15 for two.

Fresh Mint

115 Baldwin Ave, Pā'ia ☎808/579-9144. Smart, even cool, vegetarian Vietnamese restaurant. Lots of delicious noodles, stir-fries, soups, or curries, some with soy chicken or soy fish, others with tofu or just eggplant. All entrees cost around $10.

Mā'alaea Grill

Mā'alaea Harbor Village, 192 Mā'alaea Rd, Mā'alaea ☎808/243-2206. Closed for dinner on Mon. Perched above the harbor at the seaward end of Mā'alaea's central mall, with an ocean-view terrace that comes into its own at lunchtime, the *Mā'alaea Grill* serves conventional meat and seafood entrees at reasonable prices – reckon on $20 or less for a dinner entree – and specializes in salads at midday.

Mā'alaea Waterfront Restaurant

50 Hau'oli St, Mā'alaea ☎808/244-9028. Last seating 8.30pm. High-class dinner-only restaurant, in a somewhat hard-to-find location; head east – further around the bay – from the Maui Ocean Center. The menu focuses on expensive freshly caught fish, with a *cioppino* stew priced at $38, and the views are tremendous.

Mama's Fish House

799 Poho Place, Pā'ia ☎808/579-8488. Upmarket and wildly popular fish restaurant, in breezy

Central Maui PLACES

▲ PĀʻIA FISH MARKET

beachfront gardens a mile east of downtown Pāʻia. At lunch, you can opt for fish sandwiches and burgers for around $12, or go for full-scale fish entrees, each identified with the name of the fisherman who caught it. Dinner offers similar choices, along with even more fancy gourmet-Hawaiian dishes like *mahi mahi* steamed in a *ti* leaf with coconut milk, costing anything from $30 upwards. While the views are sublime, if you come after sunset you may feel you're paying premium prices for little added value.

Milagros
112 Hāna Hwy at Baldwin Ave, Pāʻia ☎808/579-8755. Friendly terrace café, serving all meals at parasol-shaded tables at Pāʻia's main intersection. Salads and deli sandwiches for around $8; burgers, tacos, and burritos for more like $10.

Moana Bakery & Cafe
71 Baldwin Ave, Pāʻia ☎808/579-9999. Smart, tasteful café/restaurant not far off the main highway, with mosaic tables and large windows. Fancy breakfasts, lunchtime *saimin* or sandwiches ($7–10), and dinner entrees ($10–26) that range from green or red Thai curries to chili-seared *ahi* to *opakapaka laulau* (snapper wrapped in *ti* leaves).

Pāʻia Fish Market
110 Hāna Hwy at Baldwin Ave, Pāʻia ☎808/579-8030. Informal, inexpensive place with wooden benches, where fresh fish – sashimi or blackened – is $13, while scallops, shrimp, and calamari cost a bit more, and a fish or meat burger is just $7. Pasta entrees include chicken ($14) and seafood ($16), and there's a sideline in quesadillas, fajitas, and soft tacos.

Kīhei

If you've always thought of Hawaii as Condo Hell, then Kīhei probably comes closer to matching that image than anywhere else in the state. Stretching for seven miles south from Māʻalaea Bay, it's a totally formless sprawl of a place, whose only landmarks consist of one dull mall or condo building after another. That said, it can be a perfectly pleasant place to spend your vacation, with abundant inexpensive lodging and dining options. It also holds plentiful beaches; each successive bay is filled with a narrow strip of white sand, so most hotels are within easy walking distance of a good stretch of beach.

Mai Poina ʻOe Iaʻu Beach County Park

The first easy point of access to the ocean along South Kīhei Road comes within a few hundred yards, at Mai Poina ʻOe Iaʻu Beach County Park. This narrow, shadeless beach is not somewhere you'd choose to spend a day, or to go swimming, but it's a good launching point for surfers, kayakers, and especially windsurfers. Māʻalaea Bay offers ideal conditions for relatively inexperienced windsurfers – and, for that matter, makes a good place for proficient sailboarders who are new to Hawaii to test the waters before venturing out into the mighty waves of Hoʻokipa (see p.123).

Hawaiian Islands Humpback Whale National Marine Sanctuary

726 S Kīhei Rd ☎808/879-2818 or 1-800/831-4888, ✆www.hihwnms .nos.noaa.gov. Mon–Sat 10am–3pm. Free. Squeezed onto a minor headland, a small compound serves as the headquarters of the Hawaiian Islands Humpback Whale National Marine Sanctuary. The organization was

created to protect and study the estimated three thousand humpback whales that annually winter in Hawaiian waters. Enthusiastic volunteers can explain its work and talk you through the displays in the garage-like Education Center. Though the organization's offices, located in the larger blue house on the seafront, are not open to the public, its spacious verandah is equipped with free binoculars and makes an ideal spot for watching whales in Māʻalaea Bay.

Kōʻieʻie Fishpond

A six-acre tract of ocean immediately offshore from the whale sanctuary headquarters is enclosed by the lava walls of the Kōʻieʻie Fishpond, which dates originally from the sixteenth century. The art of aquaculture, or fish-farming, was developed by the ancient Hawaiians to standards unmatched elsewhere in Polynesia. Such fishponds are laced around sheltered coastal areas on all the islands. The sea wall held one or two gaps, or sluice gates, which were usually sealed off with wooden lattices. Small fry could enter, but once

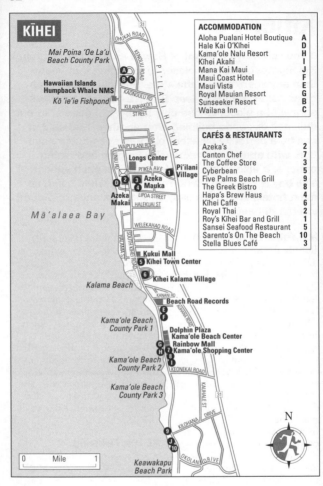

KĪHEI

OHUKAI ROAD
31
KENOLU ROAD

Mai Poina 'Oe La'u
Beach County Park

Hawaiian Islands
Humpback Whale NMS

Kō 'ie'ie Fishpond

KAONOULU RD
KULANIHAKOʻI
STREET

WAIPUʻILANI RD

Longs Center

PIʻIKEA AVE

Azeka
Mauka

LIPOA STREET

Azeka
Makai

HALEKUAI ST

WELEKAHAO ROAD

Mā'alaea Bay

Kukui Mall

Kihei Town Center

Kīhei Kalama Village

Kalama Beach

KANANI RD

Beach Road Records

Kama'ole Beach
County Park 1

Dolphin Plaza
Kama'ole Beach Center
Rainbow Mall
Kama'ole Shopping Center

Kama'ole Beach
County Park 2

KEONEKAI ROAD

Kama'ole Beach
County Park 3

KAUHALE ST

KILOHANA DRIVE

31

N

0   Mile   1

OKOLANI DRIVE

Keawakapu
Beach Park

ACCOMMODATION

Aloha Pualani Hotel Boutique	A
Hale Kai O'Kīhei	D
Kama'ole Nalu Resort	H
Kīhei Akahi	I
Mana Kai Maui	J
Maui Coast Hotel	F
Maui Vista	E
Royal Mauian Resort	G
Sunseeker Resort	B
Wailana Inn	C

CAFÉS & RESTAURANTS

Azeka's	2
Canton Chef	7
The Coffee Store	3
Cyberbean	5
Five Palms Beach Grill	9
The Greek Bistro	8
Hapa's Brew Haus	4
Kīhei Caffe	6
Royal Thai	2
Roy's Kīhei Bar and Grill	1
Sansei Seafood Restaurant	5
Sarento's On The Beach	10
Stella Blues Café	3

they grew to full size they'd be unable to leave, and it was a simple matter to harvest them in nets. Saltwater fishponds like this one, used to raise *'ama'ama* (mullet) and *awa* (milkfish), were complemented by similar freshwater ponds, usually built near rivermouths that were sealed off from the sea by sandbars, and held such species as *'ōpae* (shrimp) and *'o'opu* (a native goby).

Kalama Beach

To the naked eye, and especially to guests staying at oceanfront properties such as the *Hale Kai O' Kīhei* and its neighbors (see p.156), the beaches of northern Kīhei look attractive enough, if rather narrow. However, thanks to the output of a sewage-treatment facility here at Kalama Beach, this entire stretch is best admired from dry land; swimming is not recommended.

▲ KALAMA BEACH

Nonetheless, the large lawns and sports fields on the promontory at Kalama remain popular with locals, especially in the evenings, and there's a pretty coconut grove as well.

Kama'ole Beach County Park

Much the busiest of the Kīhei beaches – and for good reason – are the three separate, numbered segments of Kama'ole Beach County Park, immediately beyond Kalama. All boast clean white sand and are generally safe for swimming, with lovely views across the bay to West Maui, and all are supervised by lifeguards. Most of beautifully soft Kama'ole 1 beach is very close to the road, but it also curves away out of sight to the north, which is where you're likely to find the best snorkeling conditions. Little Kama'ole 2, cradled between two headlands, is a bit short on shade, and very near a large concentration of condos, which leaves long, broad Kama'ole 3 as the pick of the bunch. Families gather under the giant trees on its wide lawns, while the beach itself, which is especially popular with boogie-boarders,

is shielded from the road at the bottom of a ten-foot grassy slope.

Keawakapu Beach Park

In high season, Keawakapu Beach Park, at the far south end of South Kīhei Road, makes an inviting and less crowded alternative to Kama'ole. Swimming is best in the center, while there's good snorkeling off the rocks to the south, thanks to an artificial offshore reef made up mostly of old automobile parts that were submerged in the hope of boosting the local fish population.

Shops

Azeka Makai and Azeka Mauka

1279 and 1280 S Kīhei Rd. This matching pair of malls, the largest in Kīhei, stand across the main highway from each other. The older Azeka Makai, on the ocean side, holds the local post office, a large Bank of Hawaii with ATMs, a Crazy Shirts aloha wear store, and several fast-food places, while the smarter Azeka Mauka opposite offers more upscale eateries and a wide range of tourist-oriented stores.

▼ KAMA'OLE BEACH COUNTY PARK

Beach Road Records

2395 S Kīhei Rd ☎808/874-8863.
Lots of secondhand as well
as new CDs, and the expert
advice willingly offered make
Beach Road Records the best
place to buy Hawaiian music
on Maui; they stock other
genres as well.

Hawaiian Moons Natural Foods

Kama'ole Beach Center, 2411 S Kīhei
Rd ☎808/875-4356. Very good
wholefood store with a great
deli counter, and lots of high-
quality cosmetics and beauty
products, including island-made
sunblocks, soaps, and oils.

Kīhei Kalama Village

1945 S Kīhei Rd. Several
inexpensive restaurants–cum–
bars–cum–fast-food outlets and
a few tourist-oriented souvenir,
T-shirt, and aloha wear shops,
comprise most of what this
low-slung, open-air mall has
on offer. Its central arcade
of crafts and trinket stalls is
where you'll find Tuna Luna,
which features some interesting
creations by local Maui wood
carvers, jewelers, ceramicists,
and the like.

Cafés

The Coffee Store

Azeka Mauka, 1279 S Kīhei Rd
☎808/875-4244, ⊛www.mauicoffee
.com. Cheery mall café serving
espressos of all kinds, plus
breakfast pastries, lunch salads,
pizzas, and sandwiches.

Cyberbean

Kīhei Town Center, 1881 S Kīhei Rd
☎808/879-4799. Internet café
that, as well as specialty coffees,
provides the usual array of
inexpensive pizzas, salads, and
sandwiches.

Kīhei Caffe

1945 S Kīhei Rd ☎808/879-2230.
Friendly café offering espressos,
flavored lattes, and smoothies,
plus breakfast eggs and pancakes
and $7 lunchtime sandwiches or
burgers, to take out or eat at a
shaded roadside gazebo.

Restaurants

Azeka's

Azeka Makai, 1280 S Kīhei Rd
☎808/879-0611. Small
"local-style" snack shop and

▼ BEACH ROAD RECORDS

▲ KĪHEI CAFFE

items – mostly Pacific Rim, along with standard ribs and steaks – are delicious and beautifully presented, with appetizers such as soft-shell crab cakes in Japanese tartare sauce ($14) and entrees like fresh *opah* (moonfish), and Szechuan glazed rack of lamb ($25–39).

takeout joint, with a few tables, serving *saimin* ($3.25), plus sushi and the Hawaiian favorite *loco moco*, an egg-topped hamburger. They also sell marinated ribs, and teriyaki beef and chicken, all uncooked and ready for barbecuing; in fact, in the afternoon, they're the only things available.

Canton Chef
Kama'ole Shopping Center, 2463 S Kīhei Rd ☎808/879-1988. Roomy Chinese restaurant, with $7 lunch specials and a dinner menu bursting with chicken, shrimp, scallop, and fish entrees ($7–19.50), including several served in a tangy black-bean sauce. With advance notice, they'll prepare a whole Peking duck for $39.50. Daily 11am–2pm & 5–9pm.

Five Palms Beach Grill
Mana Kai Maui, 2960 S Kīhei Rd ☎808/879-2607. Beachfront restaurant on the ground floor of a condo building, with open terraces within earshot of the waves, and live music nightly. An à la carte brunch menu is served until 2.30pm daily, including a smoked-salmon eggs Benedict for $16, or salad or lunch specials for $10–17. Dinner

The Greek Bistro
2511 S Kīhei Rd ☎808/879-9330. Friendly, dinner-only Greek place on a garden terrace set back from the road and crammed with coconut palms and a banyan tree. Authentic appetizers like feta and olive salad, or stuffed grape leaves go for $8–10; entrees include *moussaka* and *souvlaki* for under $20, while the "Taste of Greece" mixed platter costs $23 per person.

Hapa's Brew Haus
41 E Lipoa St ☎808/879-9001. Closed Sun. Large, popular mall brewpub, whose success as a venue for live Hawaiian music – the highlight of the week is Willie K's Monday gig, though the members of Hapa play very occasionally, and there's a DJ night on Saturdays – has resulted in ever less space being devoted to its basic Mexican restaurant, where sizeable dinners cost around $10.

Roy's Kīhei Bar and Grill
Pi'ilani Village, 303 Pi'ikea Ave ☎808/891-1120. Large, lively,

Kīhei PLACES

and always busy dinner-only outlet of the upscale island chain, beside the upper highway in a mall half a mile up from Kīhei Road. Signature Roy's dishes such as lemongrass-crusted *shutome* (swordfish) and blackened rare *ahi* stream from the open kitchen, at around $10–13 for an appetizer and $25–30 for an entree. The steamed fresh catch ($29.50) is irresistible, while half a Mongolian roasted duck or honey-mustard short rib is $24.50. A five-course set menu costs $41.50.

Royal Thai

Azeka Makai, 1280 S Kīhei Rd ☏808/874-0813. Small place, tucked away at the back of the mall, serving Kīhei's best Thai food. Choose from red, yellow, and green curries in vegetarian, meat, and fish versions; *tom yum* (spicy and sour soup) and long-rice soups; and mussels in black-bean sauce – all for $8–10.

Sansei Seafood Restaurant

Kīhei Town Center, 1881 S Kīhei Rd ☏808/669-6286. Sensational Japanese–Hawaiian, dinner-only restaurant, also found in Kapalua (see p.70). Individual appetizers and entrees are invariably delicious, but the special Omakase Tasting Menu, at $65 for two, is fabulous value, offering copious portions of signature dishes such as *miso* butterfish and the Asian rock shrimp cake. It's all pretty hectic, so don't expect to linger over a romantic dinner, and there are no views, but it's a dynamic, even glamorous spot, and the food is out of this world. Laser karaoke until 2am at weekends.

▲ SANSEI SEAFOOD RESTAURANT

Sarento's On The Beach

Best Western Oceanfront Inn, 2980 S Kīhei Rd ☏808/875-7555. This dinner-only Italian restaurant is very much a special-occasion kind of place, at Kīhei's southern end in an open-sided pavilion adjoining Keawakapu Beach, which is gently spotlit once the sun goes down. Everything is scrupulously tasteful, from the complimentary focaccia bread to the Sinatra soundtrack, but with starters like gazpacho with shrimp or the house salad costing $12–15, and entrees such as tiger shrimp at over $30, or *cioppino* seafood stew for $44, the check can be gargantuan, especially if you buy your souvenir photo from the house snapper.

Stella Blues Café

Azeka Mauka, 1279 S Kīhei Rd ☏808/874-3779. California-style café, complete with ponytailed waiters and Grateful Dead posters, and centering on a huge wood-burning grill. The menu includes continental and cooked breakfasts ($6–10); burger, salad, and sandwich lunches ($8–13; try the special of grilled and roasted vegetables on herb bread); dinners like fettuccini Alfredo, Cajun chicken, crab cakes, and ribs ($14–22); as well as an assortment of smoothies and espressos.

Wailea and Mākena

With South Maui's finest beaches and most attractive
landscapes, it's by no coincidence that the resort area
of Wailea and Mākena is much more exclusive and
upscale than what's found further north at Kīhei. Brack-
eted between the velvet lawns of the golf courses that
carpet the higher slopes inland and crescent beaches of
white sand, Wailea and Mākena together are dominated
by half a dozen large and luxurious properties. Each is a
fully-fledged fantasyland containing hundreds of rooms,
several restaurants and shops, spas, tennis courts, and
vast landscaped complexes of pools and gardens. What
the resorts don't have, however, are their own private
beaches; here, like everywhere else in Hawaii, they are
public. Glorious strands like Polo and Maluaka should
not be missed, while resort development stops just
short of the best beach of all, Oneloa or Big Beach.

Ulua Beach

The northernmost access to
Wailea's beaches is provided by
a short road that leads from just
past the *Renaissance Wailea* down
to Ulua Beach. As this stretch
of coast usually experiences the
highest surf in South Maui, the
beach is popular with body-
surfers and boogie-boarders.
There's also great snorkeling
around the rocky point that
separates it from Mōkapu Beach,
a short walk to the north.

Wailea Beach

Although Wailea Beach itself,
reached by a spur road between
the *Grand Wailea*
and the *Four
Seasons*, is the most
overshadowed by
the resorts of all
the beaches in
the vicinity, the
hotels are here
for a reason. A
broad, magnificent
expanse of curving
sand, it offers safe

swimming virtually year round,
with a gentle ripple at the
southern end to please first-
time boogie-boarders, and easy
snorkeling around the rocks at
either extremity. The views are
great too, looking across the
bay with its busy pleasure-boat
traffic and whales in winter to
East Maui on the far side.

Polo Beach

Polo Beach, immediately south
of Wailea Beach, is the best of
the lot for good old-fashioned
swimming. A pleasant, paved
coastal trail connects it to
Wailea Beach, while if you're

▼ WAILEA BEACH

PLACES Wailea and Mākena

WAILEA AND MĀKENA

Mōkapu Beach Park
Wailea
Ulua Beach Park
The Shops at Wailea
Wailea Beach Park
Wailea Point
Polo Beach Park
Palauea Beach Park
Hāloa Point
Po'olenalena Beach Park
Nāhuna Point
Mākena Landing
Mākena Bay
Mākena
Keawala'i Church
Mākena Beach Park
Pu'u Ōla'i (360 ft)
Little Beach
Oneloa (Big) Beach
'Āhihi Bay

WAILEA ALANUI · WAILEA IKI DRIVE · KAUKAHI · MĀKENA ROAD · MĀKENA ALANUI · HO'OALI · KUKULANI DRIVE · PI'ILANI HIGHWAY · KA'A'AKEA DRIVE

ACCOMMODATION
Fairmont Kea Lani Maui
Four Seasons Resort Maui at Wailea — E
Grand Wailea Resort — D
Maui Prince — C
Outrigger Palms at Wailea — F
Renaissance Wailea Beach Resort — B
— A

RESTAURANTS
Caffe Ciao — 4
Hakone — 6
Joe's Bar & Grill — 1
Prince Court — 5
SeaWatch — 5
Spago — 3
Tommy Bahama's Tropical Café — 2

N
0   Mile   1

▲ POLO BEACH

driving there's plenty of parking just off Kaukahi Street, on the south side of the *Fairmont Kea Lani*. The path down from the parking lot hits the sand at Polo Beach's northern end, which, being right beneath the hotel, can feel rather a goldfish bowl, crammed with loungers and short on shade. Double back south, however, and you'll come to two much less crowded stretches, which in winter become distinct beaches.

Palauea Beach

Well away from the built-up areas, Palauea Beach is the quietest of the Wailea beaches. Surfers and boogie-boarders predominate, but it's also a good spot for a family day by the sea, and for snorkeling. In 1994, Palauea Beach was where the US Navy held a ceremony formally handing control of the island of Kaho'olawe back to the people of Hawaii.

Mākena Bay

Mākena Road, which leaves Mākena Alanui Drive a little over a mile south of the *Kea Lani*, skirts the shoreline of Mākena Bay. This was once the site of busy Mākena Landing

Kahoʻolawe

The uninhabited island of Kahoʻolawe is clearly visible from all along Maui's south and west coasts, and especially around Wailea and Mākena. Measuring just eleven miles by six, and a maximum of 1477 feet above sea level, it's the eighth largest Hawaiian island, with its nearest point a mere eight miles off Maui. From a distance, Kahoʻolawe looks like a barren hillock; at sunset it glows red, thanks to a haze of red dust lifted by the winds. Trapped in the rainshadow of Haleakalā, it receives thirty inches of rain a year. Agriculture is all but impossible, though a few green valleys, invisible from the other islands, cut into the central plateau.

During World War II, the island was appropriated by the US Navy, which used it to practice the kind of amphibious landings that ultimately ensured the defeat of Japan. After prolonged campaigning by Hawaiian activists, it was eventually handed back to the state of Hawaii in 1994. It's still, however, being cleared of unexploded ordnance, and access remains extremely restricted.

harbor, which was superseded by the creation of Kahului's new docks in the 1920s. The jetty has now gone, leaving behind a sleepy black-lava bay with little sand.

Keawalaʻi Congregational Church

Keawalaʻi Congregational Church stands on an oceanfront patch of lawn that doubles as a graveyard, surrounded by trees with multicolored blossoms. It's a plain cement structure, topped by a pretty, wood-shingled belfry, and painted with a neat green trim; the coconut palms beyond front a tiny beach. Visitors are welcome to the 7.30am and 10am Sunday services, which incorporate Hawaiian language and music.

Maluaka Beach

Keawalaʻi Church is opposite the parking lot for Maluaka Beach – also known as Mākena Beach Park, which naturally leads to confusion with Mākena State

Park – a hundred yards down the road. Though dominated somewhat by the *Maui Prince*, especially at its southern end, it remains an attractive little half-moon beach, with reasonable snorkeling. Its combination of relative tranquility and superb sunset views over Molokini and Kahoʻolawe also makes it a favorite spot for wedding ceremonies.

Oneloa Beach (Big Beach)

Maui's most spectacular sweep of golden sand stretches for over half a mile south of the landmark cinder cone of Puʻu ʻŌlaʻi, just south of Mākena. There's not a building in sight at Oneloa Beach (literally "long sand," and

▼ KEAWALAʻI CONGREGATIONAL CHURCH

widely known as Big Beach), just perfect sands and mighty surf, backed by a dry forest of *kiawe* and cacti. During the 1970s, it was home to a short-lived hippy commune; nowadays it's officially Mākena State Park, with two paved access roads.

The very first turn off the main road south of Mākena, though labeled "Mākena State Park," is a dirt track that leads via an orange gate to a scrubby gray-sand beach. Instead, keep going on the main road until you reach the paved turnoff to Oneloa, three quarters of a mile beyond the *Maui Prince*. A footpath from the parking lot here leads through the trees to a small cluster of portable toilets and picnic tables, and then emerges at the north end of Big Beach. While the clear blue ocean across this broad expanse of deep, coarse sand is irresistible, Big Beach is actually extremely dangerous, because it faces straight out to sea and lacks a reef to protect it. Huge waves crash right on to the shoreline, and fearsome rip currents tear along the coast just a few feet out. Although it's been the scene of many drownings, all lifeguards were controversially withdrawn several years ago, to cut costs.

Despite its perils, Big Beach remains busy most of the time with enthusiastic swimmers, boogie-boarders, and even snorkelers. Non-locals tend to congregate at its northern end, where in calmer periods the red-brown cliffs provide enough shelter to create a little turquoise "lagoon" of relatively placid water.

Little Beach

Walk right to the northern end of Big Beach, and, as if by magic, a natural cleft in the cliff reveals the "stairway" across the rocks that enables you to reach the much smaller, and significantly safer, Little Beach. Shielded by a rocky headland, and shaded by the adjacent trees, this is perhaps the most idyllic swimming spot on Maui, with views of Molokini and Lanai. The winter surf can still get pretty high, however, so to make the most of it it helps if you're into body-surfing.

One relic of the hippy days is that Little Beach is still widely known as an (illegal) nudist beach; even if you don't go naked yourself, some of your fellow beachgoers certainly will. As a result, they can be extremely sensitive to intruders carrying, let alone using, cameras.

▼ ONELOA BEACH

Puʻu ʻŌlaʻi

Halfway along the easy trail between Big and Little beaches, where the ground levels off at the top of the first cliff, another trail doubles back to climb Puʻu ʻŌlaʻi itself. This crumbling cinder cone was produced by one of Maui's very last volcanic eruptions, perhaps two centuries ago, and is barely held together by scrubby grass and thorns. The ascent is so steep that strongly

The first foreigner on Maui

By spending three hours ashore at the bay named after him on May 30, 1786, French Admiral Jean-François Galaup, Comte de la Pérouse, became the first foreigner to set foot on Maui. He was under orders to claim the island for the King of France but, unusually for a European, considered that he had no right to do so. His ships, the *Astrolabe* and the *Boussole,* simply sailed away, and were lost with all hands in the Solomon Islands two years later.

Before departing, La Pérouse encountered a handful of coastal villages in the area. Its inhabitants knew it as *Keone'ō'io,* or "bonefish beach," and told of how chief Kalani'opu'u of the Big Island had landed a fleet of canoes here during an attempted invasion of Maui a few years earlier. However, the villages were largely destroyed just four years after La Pérouse's visit by the last known eruption of Haleakalā. A river of lava two miles wide flowed into the sea at the center of what had been one long bay, to create the two separate bays seen today. Look inland from here to see several russet cinder cones that are relics of the eruptions.

worded signs warn against making the attempt. If you do try, you may find you have to advance on all fours. Scrambling over the raw red – and very sharp – cinders is extremely painful in anything other than proper hiking boots.

The summit of Pu'u 'Ōla'i – which is not the peak you see at the start of the climb – is a wonderful vantage point for watching humpback whales in winter. It commands views all the way up the flat coast to Wailea and Kīhei, down the full length of Big Beach, inland to the green uplands of Haleakalā, across the ocean to the low ridge of Molokini – circled by cruise boats from dawn onwards – and beyond to glowing red Kahoolawe, the West Maui Mountains, and Lanai.

La Pérouse Bay

Mākena Road continues for another three miles south from Big Beach, as a narrow, undulating road that often narrows to a single lane. During the initial stretch, it runs right beside the ocean, clinging to the coastline of 'Āhihi Bay around several small coves

lined by very rough, jagged *'a'ā* lava, before setting out across a wide, desolate field of yet more chunky lava. Secluded La Pérouse Bay, one of the island's finest snorkeling and kayaking destinations, lies beyond the parking lot at the far end. A cairn here bears a bronze plaque commemorating the voyages of the French Admiral Jean-François Galaup, Comte de la Pérouse.

'Āhihi-Kīna'u Natural Area Reserve

The waters around the headland at the east end of La Pérouse Bay are set aside as the 'Āhihi-Kīna'u Natural Area Reserve, notable for its large numbers of dolphins. All fishing is forbidden; snorkeling is allowed, but it's easier to enter the water in the inlets around La Pérouse Bay itself than to go in off the rocky headland. The very best snorkeling areas can only be reached on foot, along a trail that follows the shoreline around to the right when you reach the end of the road, to a succession of successively clearer little coves. Scuba divers too enter the water straight from the shore, most usually from 'Āhihi Bay. In addition, the kayak operators listed on p.171 run excursions here. The trail from the road meanders alternately across the sands and among the scrubby *kiawe* trees to follow the whole curve of the bay. The lichen-covered walls of ancient dwellings can often be glimpsed in the undergrowth.

Kanaio Beach

At the far end of La Pérouse Bay, you come to another field of crumbled, reddish-brown lava. A separate trail – not the obvious coastal path, which soon peters out, but one further inland – heads onwards from here. While it's of some historic interest, tracing the route of the King's Highway footpath that once ringed the entire island, it's extremely rugged, hot, and exposed. As archeologists and environmentalists alike are keen to minimize the impact of visitation on this area, it's probably best not to bother.

Shops

The Shops at Wailea

3750 Wailea Alanui Drive, Wailea ☎808/891-6770, ⊛www .shopsatwailea.com. The proximity of so many big-spending tourists has ensured the rapid growth of the Shops at Wailea to become Maui's most upscale shopping mall. Its ideal target audience can readily be divined from the presence of Louis Vuitton, Cartier, and Dolce & Gabbana outlets, but it also holds plenty of stores aimed at more ordinary folk, including Honolua Surf Co for surf and aloha wear; Martin and MacArthur for top-notch Hawaiian crafts and playful *tiki* souvenirs; Footprints; Banana

Republic; and a well-stocked Ritz Camera, the island's best camera store.

Restaurants

Caffe Ciao

Fairmont Kea Lani, 4100 Wailea Alanui Drive, Wailea ☎808/875-2225. Very good, if pricey, Italian bakery/ deli/trattoria, downstairs and to the left of the *Kea Lani*'s imposing lobby. The deli section sells pastries and espressos all day, plus massive doorstep sandwiches like a hummus wrap for $8.50 or a pesto sandwich for $9, while the trattoria serves more formal meals on an open-air terrace, with lunchtime panini sandwiches or pasta specials for $14–20, and dinners ranging from $17–19 pizzas up to a $31 veal saltimbocca or a $36 *cioppino* seafood stew.

▼ SHOPS AT WAILEA

▲ CAFFE CIAO

Hakone

Maui Prince, 5400 Mākena Alanui
Drive, Mākena ☎808/875-5888.
Closed Sun. Classic dinner-only
Japanese restaurant, upstairs
in the *Prince*, with tastefully
minimal decor – but for the odd
framed vintage Aloha shirt – and
no views. On Mondays, there's a
$45 dinner buffet; otherwise the
seven-course Rakuen Kaiseki
set menu costs $60, but you
can also order sushi or sashimi
dinners for around $40, smaller
set menus for more like $35, or
simply individual dishes from
the sushi bar.

Joe's Bar & Grill

131 Wailea Iki Place, Wailea
☎808/875-7767. Open daily for
dinner only. One of Maui's most
fashionable restaurants, owned
by the same top-notch team
as the *Hali'imaile General Store*
(see p.111). Neither the tennis-
club setting nor the decor
– dull rock-music memorabilia
– will grab you, but the food
is heavenly, a fusion of cutting-
edge Pacific Rim cuisine with
down-home local favorites.
Appetizers ($8–20) include *ahi*

tartare with *wasabi aioli*, while
entrees ($20 and up) range from
meatloaf with garlic mashed
potatoes to a smoky, applewood-
grilled salmon.

Prince Court

Maui Prince, 5400 Mākena Alanui
Drive, Mākena ☎808/875-5888.
Relatively formal, somewhat
solemn resort restaurant.
Appetizers include oysters on
the half-shell ($14), and a tower
of Hawaiian tuna and foie gras
($14). Apart from fish dishes like
the tempura *moi* (threadfish)
for $28, the entrees tend to
be rather predictable, though
caramelized Maui onions lift
options like roast lamb or
venison. Sunday morning sees
a buffet brunch for $43, and
Friday night a prime rib and
seafood buffet, also costing $43.

SeaWatch

100 Wailea Golf Club Drive, Wailea
☎808/875-8080. Grand terrace
restaurant in the clubhouse of the
Wailea Golf Club, a few hundred
yards uphill from the highway,
open daily for all meals and
enjoying stupendous ocean views

▲ MAUI SUNSET LŪʻAU

during daylight hours. Lunch is the best time to come, with well-priced specials like the $9 *kālua* pork sandwich; at night the cuisine is Pacific Rim, with $8–15 appetizers such as five-spice crab cakes, and $24–30 entrees including fish, grilled chicken, and lamb with onion torte.

Spago

Four Seasons, 3900 Wailea Alanui Drive, Wailea ☎808/879-2999. Celebrity chef Wolfgang Puck spreads himself a little thinly these days, but as befits the stunning ocean-view location in this grandest of resorts, the buzzy, glamorous *Spago* pulls out all the stops. It serves dinner only, with an assured and irresistible Pacific Rim menu that includes a great Thai lobster soup with coconut and *galangal* ($13), delicious *ahi* poke (spicy cubes of raw tuna) served in sesame *miso* cones ($16), and entrees like whole Kauai steamed *moi* (threadfish) for $33, or grilled lamb chops with chili-mint vinaigrette for $39.

Tommy Bahama's Tropical Café

The Shops at Wailea, 3750 Wailea Alanui Drive, Wailea ☎808/875-9983. Bar and restaurant adjoining the upscale clothes store of the same name. Lunch is a good value, with huge fishy sandwiches or pasta specials for $10–13 – try the tasty Habana Cubana barbecue pork sandwich – along with sweeping (if distant) ocean views from the terrace. The dinner entrees are more overtly Caribbean, including Jamaican spiced pork in rum sauce ($29) and Trinidad tuna with cilantro and lemongrass ($31).

Shows

Maui Sunset Lūʻau

Maui Prince, 5400 Mākena Alanui Drive, Mākena ☎808/875-5888. Tues, Thurs & Sat 5.30pm. $72. Although none of South Maui's *lūʻaus* is as good as the Royal Lahaina Lūʻau or the Feast at Lele in Lahaina – see p.59 – the expansive lawns of the *Maui Prince* make a great venue for an evening of eating Hawaiian foods, drinking cocktails, and watching – and even participating in – *hula* performances. The emphasis is more on partying than on presenting authentic Polynesian culture.

Upcountry Maui

Occupying the lower western slopes of Haleakalā, Upcountry Maui enjoys a deliciously temperate climate a couple of thousand feet above the isthmus. Although most visitors, drawn onwards up the mountain, don't linger here, it's among the most striking regions in all Hawaii, with lush orchards and rainforests around Makawao in the north giving way to the parched cattle country of 'Ulupalakua Ranch twenty miles to the south. It holds few significant towns and even fewer tourist attractions, and visitor accommodation is limited to a handful of small-scale B&Bs. Instead, the upcountry is marked by small farms-cum-gardens – particularly in the area of Kula – which are famous for their flowering plants, especially dazzling protea blossoms, and consistently superb views back over the isthmus, to the ocean and the West Maui Mountains.

Makawao

The small town of Makawao, seven miles up from coastal Pā'ia (see p.87), represents Maui at its best. Still recognizable as the village built by plantation workers and *paniolo* cowboys in the nineteenth century, it's now home to an active artistic community dominated by exiles from California. When they're not giving each other classes in yoga, feng shui, belly dancing, and Hawaiian healing, they make its galleries, crafts stores, and coffee bars some of the liveliest hangouts on the island.

Although Makawao extends for well over a mile, only its central intersection – where Baldwin Avenue, climbing from Pā'ia, meets Makawao Avenue from Pukalani – holds any great interest. Baldwin here points straight up Haleakalā, drawing the eye towards the lush green meadows on the slopes above town. Its timber-frame buildings, painted in fading pastel hues, are connected by a rudimentary

boardwalk and hold half a dozen quirky art galleries. The real artistic epicenter of town, however, is the Hui No'eau Visual Arts Center, a country estate a mile south at 2841 Baldwin Ave (Mon–Sat 10am–4pm; ☎808/572-6560, Ⓦwww.huinoeau.com). As well

▼ MAKAWAO

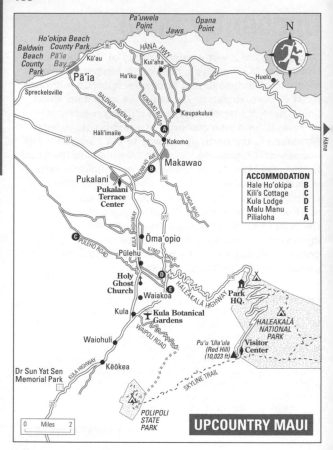

ACCOMMODATION

Hale Ho'okipa	B
Kili's Cottage	C
Kula Lodge	D
Malu Manu	E
Pilialoha	A

UPCOUNTRY MAUI

as offering classes in practical arts and crafts, it houses its own small store and a gallery for temporary exhibitions.

Makawao's *paniolo* days are commemorated on July 4 each year by the Makawao Rodeo, which includes a parade through town as well as competitive events at the Oskie Rice Arena.

Pukalani

The shapeless sprawl known as Pukalani is home to six thousand people, but has no appreciable downtown area. As a

bypass now carries traffic around rather than through it, there's no real reason for tourists ever to see the town at all. However, the run-down Pukalani Terrace Center mall holds the closest gas station to the summit of Haleakalā, as well as a big Foodland supermarket, a *Subway* sandwich shop, and several budget diners.

Holy Ghost Church

The lower upcountry road, the Kula Highway, passes just below the white octagonal

Holy Ghost Church. Portuguese Catholics came to Maui from 1878 onwards, and by 1894 were prosperous enough to construct their own church, shipping the hand-carved high-relief gilt altar from Austria, and capping the structure with a gleaming silver-roofed belfry. The interior is very light, with pink-painted walls, and features the Stations of the Cross labeled in Portuguese. Not surprisingly, this was the only octagonal structure built in nineteenth-century Hawaii; it's thought to be eight-sided either because the crown of the Portuguese Queen Isabella was octagonal, or because the German parish priest came from near Aachen, the site of a similar octagonal chapel built by Charlemagne.

Kula Botanical Garden

638 Kekaulike Hwy, Kula ☎808/878-1715. Daily 9am–4pm. $5, kids 6–12 $1. A couple of miles beyond the foot of Haleakalā Crater Road, the Kula Botanical Garden offers enjoyable self-guided tours through large and colorful landscaped gardens. Among its broad range of plants are proteas, hydrangeas, lurid yellow and red canna, and spectacular purple and yellow birds of paradise from South Africa. Many of its species betray their Pacific origins by bearing the Latin name *banksia*, in honor of Sir Joseph Banks, the pioneering botanist who sailed with Captain Cook; perhaps the finest is the red and white "Raspberry Frost" from Australia.

Polipoli State Park

Although Maui residents rave about thickly wooded Polipoli State Park, set high above the upcountry, visitors from beyond Hawaii may feel that as an "ordinary" temperate forest it holds little they can't see at home. That said, the drive up is fun, taking you off the beaten track into Maui's remoter reaches.

Polipoli Park stands at the top of the ten-mile Waipoli Road – *not* nearby Polipoli Road, oddly enough – which climbs away from Kekaulike Highway just south of the Kula Botanical Gardens. The first six miles, in which you do all the climbing, are paved, passing through tough, springy ranchland where cattle graze on the open range. This is Maui's best launching spot for hang gliders, which you may see sharing the winds with circling Hawaiian owls (rare among owls in that they fly by day, rather than night).

It shouldn't be too difficult to coax a rental car along the rough, but level, dirt road that meanders along the hillside above the ranch. After three miles, the road surface improves; drop right at the fork half a mile further along, and after

▼ HOLY GHOST CHURCH

another half a mile you'll come to Polipoli's campground in a grassy clearing, which offers neither showers nor drinking water. Tent camping here ($5), and overnight stays in the simple cabin nearby ($45 for up to four people; closed Tues), can be arranged through the state parks office in Wailuku (see p.160).

The entire Polipoli area was planted with Californian redwood trees by the Civilian Conservation Corps during the 1930s. The Redwood Trail, which leads down from a hundred yards before the campground, burrows through such thick forest that the persistent rain can barely penetrate it, and very little light does either. The forest floor is too gloomy even to support a light scattering of moss, and many of the tightly packed trees are dead. It comes as a huge relief when the trail emerges from the bottommost strip of eucalyptus after 1.5 miles to show expansive views across the ranchlands.

The Skyline Trail

Various other trails crisscross throughout Polipoli, including some to lava caves hidden in the woods, but the only one likely to interest visitors from outside Hawaii is the Skyline Trail. This epic thirteen-mile trek follows the southwest rift zone of Haleakalā right the way up to Science City, at the summit (see p.117). It climbs a dirt track that heads off to the left two miles along the left fork from the junction 9.5 miles up Waipoli Road, described above. Unless you arrange a pick-up at the far end, it's too far for a day-hike, and the higher you get the more exposed to the biting winds you'll be. Alternatively, you can take a mountain bike along the trail.

Kēōkea

A couple of miles south of the intersection of the Kekaulike and Kula highways, the village of Kēōkea consists of a small cluster of roadside stores, together with the green and

▼ POLIPOLI STATE PARK

white St John's Episcopal Church. All were built at the end of the nineteenth century to serve the local Chinese community, which also supported three Chinese-language schools and, it's said, a number of opium dens. Alongside *Grandma's Coffee Store* (see p.110), one room of Henry Fong's general store houses the appealing little Kēōkea Gallery (Tues–Sat 9am–5pm, Sun 9am–3pm), where you'll find arts and crafts displayed.

The wife and children of Sun Yat Sen, the first President of China, stayed on his brother's ranch here during 1911 and 1912, while Sun was away fomenting revolution. Hence the statue of Sun, flanked by two Chinese dragons, that looks out over Wailea and Kahoolawe from the somewhat neglected Dr Sun Yat Sen Memorial Park, which lies at the intersection of Hwy-37 and Kealakapu Road, less than two miles beyond Kēōkea.

Thanks to its healthy elevation, Kēōkea was also the site of Kula Sanatorium, which opened in 1910 to treat tuberculosis sufferers, and was soon joined by a "Preventorium" that set out to reduce the incidence of the disease.

'Ulupalakua Ranch

Six miles south from Kēōkea, the six tin-roofed, single-story wooden buildings of the 'Ulupalakua Ranch headquarters nestle into a shady bend in the road. Comings and goings are overseen by the three carved wooden cowboys stationed permanently on the porch of the 'Ulupalakua Ranch Store (daily 9am–4.30pm); inside, you can buy simple lunches, including burgers made from the ranch's own cattle, plus *paniolo* hats, T-shirts, and limited basic supplies.

'Ulupalakua Ranch started out in the middle of the nineteenth century as Rose Ranch, owned by an ex-whaling captain, James McKee. Originally its main business was sugar, but the focus soon shifted to cattle, and it employed expert *paniolo* cowboys such as Ike Purdy, a former world rodeo champion. In his huge mansion, McKee played host to Robert Louis Stevenson and King David Kalākaua among others, who took advantage of Hawaii's first ever swimming pool. Spotting ships arriving at Mākena Landing (see p.98), McKee would fire a cannon to signal that he was sending a carriage down to meet his guests. The mansion burned down during the 1970s, but the ranch itself is still going, raising elk and sheep as well as cattle.

As detailed on p.173, the ranchlands can also be explored on off-road tours, which start here and operate under the name of Maui ATV Tours.

Tedeschi Winery

Kula Hwy, 'Ulupalakua ☏ 877/878-6058, ◍ www.mauiwine.com. Store and museum daily 9am–5pm; free tours daily 10.30am & 1.30pm.

Around the corner beyond 'Ulupalakua Ranch, one of the ranch's co-owners has established the Tedeschi Winery as a successful sideline on the site of James McKee's original Rose Ranch. It uses two annual grape harvests from a small vineyard in a fold below the highway, a mile to the north, to produce 30,000 cases a year of white, red, and rosé wines, as well as *Maui Brut* champagne and sweet, dry, and even sparkling pineapple wines. They're on sale in the King's

▲ TEDESCHI WINERY

Cottage, which also houses an entertaining little museum of ranch and cowboy history, and serves as the assembly point for fifteen-minute guided tours. The converted and imitation ranch buildings used for processing and bottling are less than enthralling, but you do at least get to see some amazing trees, including a pine drowning in multicolored creeping bougainvillea, and a giant camphor.

Pi'ilani Highway

South of 'Ulupalakua, Kula Highway confusingly becomes the Pi'ilani Highway, despite having no connection with the parallel road of the same name that runs through Wailea and Mākena down below. For all the strictures of the rental companies – see p.164 – it takes appalling weather to render it unsafe, and for most of the year it's possible to drive all the way along the south coast to Hāna, 37 miles away. A detailed description of the route, coming in the opposite direction, begins on p.140.

Cafés

Café del Sol

3620 Baldwin Ave, Makawao ☎808/572-4877. Off-street daytime café in Makawao's Courtyard Mall, serving espressos, pastries, salads, sandwiches, and blue plate specials, all for under $10, at shaded garden tables.

Duncan's Coffee Co

3647 Baldwin Ave, Makawao ☎808/573-9075. Smart little coffee place on the main drag, with paninis, espressos, and smoothies, and even a little sushi bar.

Grandma's Coffee Store

Kula Hwy, Kēōkea ☎808/878-2140. While you're unlikely to see "Grandma" herself at this village café, there's plenty of fresh Maui-grown coffee, plus avocado sandwiches, salads, macnut pesto, taro burgers, and killer homemade cookies or desserts such as blueberry cobbler.

Restaurants

Casanova's

1188 Makawao Ave, Makawao ☎808/572-0220, ◉www .casanovamaui.com. The 1970s Art Nouveau–style lettering and faded exterior of this single-story wooden building in the heart of Makawao belies its status as one of Maui's hottest nightspots. There's a dance floor and bar just inside the door, a romantic Italian restaurant stretches further back, and the breakfast deli/espresso bar is alongside. Lunchtime salads, pastas, and sandwiches range from $6 to $15, while in the evening, wood-fired pizzas cost $10–18, pasta entrees are $12–18, and specials are $20–25. Portions are huge. The $5 cover charge on dance nights (unless you dine) can rise to $10 when there's live music (typically Fri and Sat).

Hali'imaile General Store

900 Hali'imaile Rd, Hali'imaile ☎808/572-2666. One of Maui's very best restaurants, serving gourmet Hawaiian food in a large, bright, and smart former store in the village of Hali'imaile, which is two miles down Baldwin Avenue from Makawao and then a mile west towards Haleakalā Highway. Appetizers (up to $20) include an Asian pear and duck taco, and fresh island fish cakes; entrees, like Szechuan barbecued salmon or rack of lamb Hunan style, can cost over $30; and there's also a raw bar. Lunch is served on weekdays only.

Kitada's Saimin

3617 Baldwin Ave, Makawao ☎808/572-7241. Closed Sun. Very old-fashioned local-style diner, open from dawn until lunchtime only. $5 buys a huge bowl of *saimin*, while burgers, sandwiches, and plate lunches cost little more.

▼ CASANOVA'S

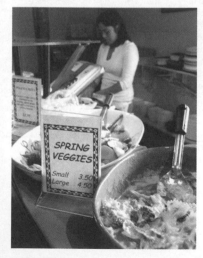

SPRING VEGGIES
Small 3.50
Large 4.50

Kula Lodge

Haleakalā Hwy, Kula ☎808/878-1535, ⊛www.kulalodge.com. Daily 6.30am–9pm. The wood-furnished dining room of *Kula Lodge* is open until the evening, but it's busiest at the start of the day, when most of the customers are already on their way back *down* Haleakalā. The food is American, with a definite Pacific Rim tinge; the lunch menu consists of sandwiches, burgers, and a few selections from the dinner menu ($9–15), while evening offerings include a *miso* oysters Rockefeller appetizer ($14), and lamb *osso buco* or *lilikoi* prawns (around $30). Protea blossoms adorn the tables, and the views are immense.

Kula Sandalwoods

15427 Haleakalā Hwy, Kula ☎808/878-3523. Home-grown upcountry produce forms the basis of the menu at this attractive little restaurant, on the *mauka* (mountain) side of the highway just before Haleakalā Crater Road heads off towards the summit. Open for breakfast and lunch only, with waffles and omelets earlier on replaced by $8–13 lunch specials including soup and sandwiches.

Polli's

1202 Makawao Ave, Makawao ☎808/572-7808. Busy, good-value Mexican restaurant at Makawao's central crossroads, open for all meals daily. All the usual menu items are on offer, from chimichangas to fajitas (under $10), and they also do barbecue chicken and ribs on Mondays.

Haleakalā

Although the mighty volcano Haleakalā dominates Maui, it's hard to appreciate its full majesty until you climb right to the top. Around a million people each year make the journey, with many timing their ascent to coincide with the dawn, when the sun rises above the far side of the crater – but don't imagine that it's not worth coming later in the day. Winding Haleakalā Highway provides the only route, climbing more than ten thousand feet above sea level in a mere 38 miles. Beyond the verdant upcountry, it leads through purple-blossoming jacaranda, firs, and eucalyptus to reach open ranching land, then sweeps in huge curves to awe-inspiring Haleakalā Crater itself. This eerie wasteland makes a superb spectacle at any time of day, but best of all is mid-afternoon, when the sun lights up its staggering array of russet cinder cones, ashen slopes, pockmarked craters, and craggy cliffs.

The summit drive

From all the major accommodation centers on Maui, the quickest route to the top of Haleakalā is to head for Kahului, and then follow Haleakalā Highway into the upcountry. From there, only Haleakalā Crater Road continues all the way to the summit, entering the park after a twisting twelve-mile climb through the meadows, reaching the park headquarters shortly after that, and ending at the summit a further ten miles on.

If you join the majority in attempting to drive up to Haleakalā Crater in time for the dawn – which varies between 5.50am in summer and 6.50am in winter – be prepared for a very early start and a long hard drive in the dark; allow two full hours to get to the top from Lahaina, Kā'anapali, or Kīhei, or one and a half hours from Kahului

or Wailuku. If you end up late for the sunrise, be warned that you'll be driving straight into the dazzling sun, and watch out for the endless posses of downhill bikers coming the other way.

Before setting out, keep in mind that the last gas station before the summit is at Pukalani, 28 miles below; the last food and lodging is at *Kula Lodge* (see p.158), 22 miles short.

Hosmer Grove and Waikamoi Preserve

Just beyond the park entrance a short road off to the left leads to the park's main campground, at Hosmer Grove. Set almost exactly at the mountain's tree line, is a pleasant wooded copse, though it marks the failure of an early twentieth-century experiment to assess Maui's suitability for timber farming. Out of almost a hundred different tree species planted by Ralph Hosmer, only twenty

Haleakalā National Park practicalities

Entrance and fees

Haleakalā National Park remains open around the clock; $5 per pedestrian or cyclist, $10 per vehicle, or $20 annual fee; national passes are sold here and valid for admission.

The park headquarters

The park headquarters looks out across central Maui from the left of the highway, three quarters of a mile up from the park entrance (daily 8am–4pm; ☎808/572-4400 information, ☎808/871-5054 weather, ⊛www.nps.gov/hale). This is the place to enquire about the day's quota of camping places, or to register if you've managed to reserve a cabin. It holds little by way of exhibits or printed information, but you can pick up a basic park brochure and buy detailed hiking maps.

Staying in the park

Hosmer Grove is the only Haleakalā campground accessible by car, and the only one for which campers do not need to obtain permits. Wilderness camping is not permitted anywhere in the park. There are, however, three rudimentary, but sound, backcountry cabins within Haleakalā Crater, which can only be reached on foot. All are on the grassy fringes of the crater, sheltered by the high surrounding cliffs, and are padlocked to deter casual backpackers from wandering in. Each is rented to one group only per night, and has twelve bunk beds, with no bedding, plus a kitchen, a stove for heating, and an outhouse. Hōlua and Palikū cabins offer tent camping in the adjacent meadows – the 25 daily permits are issued on a first-come, first-served basis at the park headquarters, between 8am and 3pm daily – but Kapalaoa Cabin does not. Water is normally available, but it's up to you to purify it before you drink it.

For complete details on cabin reservations, which require a minimum two-month advance booking, contact ☎808/572-4400 or ⊛www.nps.gov/hale/pages/tier_two/cabins.htm.

Outfitters

Companies that offer "downhill biking" trips down Haleakalā are listed on p.171, while horse-riding expeditions in the crater are listed on p.172.

survived, though that's enough to provide a nice thirty-minute nature trail.

By way of contrast, Waikamoi Preserve, adjoining Hosmer Grove, is a five-thousand-acre tract of upland rainforest that's home to a wide assortment of indigenous Hawaiian birds. You can only hike through it with an authorized guide, so call ahead to see when the next of the Park Service's regular free Waikamoi Cloud Forest Hikes is

scheduled (see above for contact details).

There's tent camping in a soft sloping meadow surrounded by tall pines; a small open pavilion holds basic washing facilities. Sites are available on a first-come, first-served basis. No advance reservations are taken, and no permit is required, but there's a three-night maximum stay. It's possible to walk all the way into Haleakalā Crater from Hosmer Grove; a supply trail

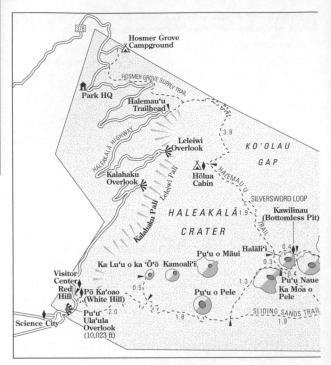

up the mountain meets the Halemauʻu Trail after 2.5 miles, just short of the crater rim.

▼ HOSMER GROVE

Halemauʻu Trailhead

Haleakalā Crater Road, 2.5 miles up from the park headquarters. Three approaches, each marked by a parking lot, lead into the crater beyond the park headquarters. The first of these, the Halemauʻu Trailhead, signals the start of one of the park's two main hiking trails, but there's nothing to see at the parking lot. The edge of the *pali*, where the trail actually drops into the crater, is almost a mile away.

Leleiwi Overlook

4.5 miles from the park headquarters. Set a couple of hundred yards beyond its parking lot, Leleiwi Overlook offers views across the isthmus to West Maui, as well as a first glimpse into Haleakalā Crater, but you'll probably have

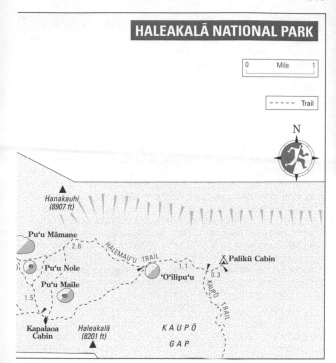

seen enough of West Maui from the Crater Road, and better vantage points over the crater lie ahead.

Kalahaku Overlook

It's only legal to stop at the Kalahaku or "Silversword" Overlook, a couple of miles short of the visitor center, as you drive down rather than up the mountain; in fact it's easy to pass by without noticing it at all. That's a shame, because this sheltered viewpoint provides perhaps the best overall prospect of Haleakalā Crater. Mauna Kea on

the Big Island is often visible through the Kaupō Gap in the ridge to the right, and when the clouds clear you can also see down to the north coast of Maui. Unless you hike into the crater, this may be the only place you see any silverswords; in theory, there should be a few

▼ LELEIWI OVERLOOK

The geology of Haleakalā

Dramatic, multicolored Haleakalā Crater, 10,023 feet above sea level at the summit of Haleakalā, and measuring more than seven miles long, two miles wide, and half a mile deep, is often hailed as the largest extinct volcanic crater in the world. As far as geologists are concerned, however, it's none of these things. Not only is the "crater" not a crater at all – in shape, size, origin, and location it bears no relation to any summit crater Haleakalā may once have possessed – but strictly speaking it's not even volcanic, having been created by erosion rather than eruption.

Fueled by the same "hot spot" that has created all the volcanoes of Hawaii, Haleakalā originally thrust its way from the ocean around 800,000 years ago. In the 400,000 years that followed, it first fused with, and eventually came to dominate, the West Maui Mountains. At its highest, it may have stood 15,000 feet tall, which is higher than Mauna Kea and Mauna Loa on the Big Island today.

The volcano then slumbered for several hundred thousand years, during which time torrential rainfall eroded away its topmost 6000 feet, and sculptured vast canyons into its flanks. Two of these valleys, Keanae to the north and Kaupō to the east, cut so deeply into the mountain that they met in the middle, creating a huge central depression. When the "hot spot" beneath Haleakalā finally reawakened, a series of smaller eruptions poured another 3000 feet of lava into that cavity, and gushed out of the Koʻolau and Kaupō gaps to refill the valleys. Peppering the summit with raw red cones of cindery ash, it made it look to the untrained eye like the sort of crater you might expect to find at the top of a volcano.

in the small enclosure below the parking lot, across from the overlook.

Haleakalā Visitor Center

Eleven miles from the park entrance. Summer daily 6am–3pm; winter daily 6.30am–3pm. No phone. Although the highway continues beyond it, most visitors consider they've reached the top of Haleakalā when they pull in at the Visitor Center. The railed open-air viewing area beside the parking lot commands great views of Haleakalā Crater. In the pre-dawn chill, however, many people prefer to admire the procession of red-brown cinder cones, marching across the moonscape far below, through the panoramic windows of the small visitor center itself. If you're feeling more energetic, follow the short paved trail to the right instead, which leads up Pa Kaʻoao, or White Hill, for 360° views.

The exhibits inside the visitor center are pretty minimal, though there's a good 3-D model of Haleakalā to help you get oriented. Park rangers also provide hiking tips and lead free guided hikes, such as the Cinder Desert walk, which sets off from here along the Sliding Sands Trail and the

▼ PUʻU ULAʻULA

▲ SCIENCE CITY

Waikamoi Cloud Forest Hike from Hosmer Grove. Call the park headquarters for current schedules (see box, p.113).

Pu'u Ula'ula (Red Hill)

A few hundred yards up from the visitor center along the highway. A smaller parking lot at a final loop in the road stands just below Pu'u Ula'ula, or Red Hill – at 10,023 feet, the highest spot on Maui. A circular shelter at the top of a short stairway offers what feel like aerial views of Haleakalā Crater. In clear conditions – soon after dawn is the best bet – you may be able to see not only the 80 miles to Mauna Loa on the Big Island, but even the 130 miles to Oahu.

Confusingly, the peak that officially bears the name of Haleakalā is five miles east, above Kapalaoa Cabin, and a couple of thousand feet lower.

Science City

The road beyond Pu'u Ula'ula is closed to the public, but leads in a few more yards to the gleaming white domes of Kolekole or Science City. This multinational astronomic research facility, perched at the top of the House of the Sun, monitors the earth's distance from the moon by bouncing laser signals off a prism left there by the Apollo astronauts.

The Sliding Sands Trail

Beginning at the visitor center parking lot, Sliding Sands Trail briefly parallels the road to skirt White Hill. It then starts its leisurely switchback sweep into the crater, down a long scree slope of soft red ash. While the *pali* to the north of the visitor center is scattered with buttresses of rock and patches of green vegetation, this side is almost completely barren, the smooth crumbling hillside only interrupted by an occasional bush. Far ahead, mists and clouds stream into the crater through the Ko'olau Gap.

It takes a while to appreciate the immensity of the crater; for the first mile, you expect to arrive at the crater floor at a

Hiking in the crater

The only way to get a real sense of the beauty and diversity of Haleakalā Crater is by hiking down into it. Although there are just two principal trails – the Sliding Sands and Halemau'u trails – the terrain varies far more than you could ever tell from the crater-edge viewpoints, ranging from forbidding desert to lush mountain meadows.

The obvious problem is that, once you've descended into the crater, you'll have to climb back out again, which at an altitude of 10,000 feet is never less than grueling. That said, reasonably fit hikers should be able to manage a day-hike that takes them down one trail and back up the other – a minimum distance of eleven miles, which is likely to take at least seven hours. More ambitiously, you could aim to take in Kapalaoa Cabin along the way, for a total of thirteen miles and more like eight hours, but heading any further east would be unrealistic. The easier route is to go down Sliding Sands and back on Halemau'u, though since the trailheads are several miles apart, you'll need to arrange a pickup or hitch a ride between the two. A parking lot for hitchhikers near the Halemau'u Trailhead (see p.114) makes it relatively easy to get a lift up the mountain.

If you've arranged to stay overnight in the crater, you could see the whole thing in two days, although most hikers spend longer. It takes a hardy and very well-prepared backpacker, however, to trek out via the Kaupō Trail to the south.

Don't underestimate the effects of the altitude. Allow an hour or so in the summit area to acclimatize before you set off on the trails; not only will that prepare you for the effort ahead, but it will also mean that you're still close to the road if you start to feel ill. By far the most effective treatment for altitude sickness is to descend a few thousand feet. Scuba divers should not go up Haleakalā within 24 hours of a dive; ask your dive operator for detailed advice.

In addition, with Haleakalā being such an ecologically delicate area, it's essential to practice minimum-impact hiking. Carry out everything you carry in, take all the water you need (reckon on three quarts a person a day), and stick to established trails. Above all, never walk on the cinder soil surrounding a silversword plant.

group of multicolored rocks in the middle distance, but when you reach them you find a longer descent ahead.

Two miles down, the trail passes between a clump of twenty-foot-high 'a'ā rock

outcroppings. A spur trail from here leads 0.4 miles, by way of a miniature "garden" of silverswords, to the smooth lip of the Ka Lu'u O Ka 'Ō'ō Crater. This full round cinder cone, glinting with pink, red, yellow, and ochre highlights in the bright sun, cradles a hollow core filled with tumbled boulders. From the trail above, you can see long clinker flows extending for two miles north of it, eating away

▼ SLIDING SANDS TRAIL

▲ HALEMAU'U TRAIL

at the neighboring Kamaoli'i Crater.

Continuing on the main trail, you wind down through a rough field of 'a'ā lava. In season, the silverswords that almost line the path shoot up above head height. For the final stretch of the total 3.8-mile descent, the desolate crater floor spreads out broad and flat ahead of you, punctuated by heaped mounds of ash.

You'll know you've reached the crater floor when you strike the south end of the clearly marked spur trail that connects the two main trails. Turning left towards the Halemau'u Trail involves a fairly stiff climb across the flanks of the ruddy Ka Moa O Pele cinder cone; over to the right, the triangular mountain peak of Hanakauhi can be seen rising beyond Pu'u Naue.

The Halemau'u Trail

The alternative route down into the crater, the switchbacking Halemau'u Trail starts at a trailhead half a dozen miles down Haleakalā Crater Road from the visitor center. Towards the end of the relatively featureless 0.75-mile descent from the parking lot to the crater rim, the main trail is joined by a side trail up from Hosmer Grove. Eventually the trail crosses a high, narrow ridge; provided the afternoon clouds aren't passing over it, you'll get staggering views down to the North Maui coastline, as well as south into the crater.

Only the first few switchbacks cross back and forth between the north and south sides of the high bluff. Here at the tip of the Leleiwi Pali, it's very obvious how the landscape below has simply poured down through the Ko'olau Gap, from the crater towards the ocean. Soon, however, the trail narrows to drop sharply down the south side of the *pali*; it never feels too dangerous, though the drop-offs are enormous. The tiny shape of the overnight Hōlua cabin comes into view a couple of miles ahead, a speck at the foot of the mighty cliff.

The trail levels out beyond a gate at the bottom of the final switchback, then undulates its

Silverswords

Haleakalā is a treasure trove of unique plants, birds, and animals, but the most distinctive of all its species is the silversword. A distant relative of the sunflower, presumably descended from a lone seed that wafted across the Pacific from America, this extraordinary plant has adapted perfectly to the forbidding conditions of Haleakalā Crater.

Known by the ancient Hawaiians as the 'āhinahina, or "silvery-gray," it consists of a gourd-shaped bowl of curving gray leaves, a couple of feet across, and cupped to collect what little moisture is available. Slender roots burrow in all directions just below the surface of the low-quality cinder soil; merely walking nearby can crush the roots and kill the plant.

Each silversword takes between three and twenty years to grow to full size, and then blossoms only once. Between May and June of the crucial year, a central shaft rises like a rocket from the desiccated silver leaves, reaching a height of from three to eight feet, and erupting with hundreds of reddish-purple flowers. These peak in July and August, releasing their precious cargo of seeds, and the entire plant then withers and dies.

way through a meadow filled with misshapen and overgrown spatter cones towards Hōlua Cabin, just under four miles from the trailhead. A slight detour is required to reach the cabin itself, where the lawns are often filled with honking nēnē geese. Beyond it, the trail climbs on to a much more rugged 'a'ā lava flow, the youngest in the crater area. Indentations in the rocky outcrops are scattered with red-berried 'ōhelo bushes, nurtured by the wet clouds that drift in through the Ko'olau Gap.

As you climb slowly towards the heart of Haleakalā Crater, you can branch away to the left to follow the brief Silversword Loop, which holds the park's greatest concentration of silversword plants.

The crater floor

At the point where the Halemau'u Trail reaches the crater floor, almost six miles from its start, a bench enables weary hikers to catch their breath while contemplating the onward haul around the north side of the Halāli'i cinder cone. If you continue south, and turn right after 0.3 miles, you'll come to the foot of the Sliding Sands Trail 1.3 miles after that.

Keep going to the left, however, and within a couple of hundred yards the Halemau'u Trail follows the crest of a low ridge to make a serpentine twist between Halali'i and the nameless cinder cone to the north. Known as Pele's Paint Pot, this gorgeous stretch is the most spectacular part of Haleakalā Crater, the trail standing out as a lurid red streak of sand against the brown and yellow mounds to either side. You can tell that Halāli'i is of relatively recent origin by the fact that its rim has not yet worn smooth; look back to see the park visitor center framed far away on the crater rim.

It's possible to loop right around Halāli'i and head back along either trail, but the Halemau'u Trail continues east for another four miles. Immediately north of the junction where you're forced to decide, you'll see the fenced-off hole of Kawilinau, also known, misleadingly, as the Bottomless Pit; in fact, this small volcanic vent is just 65 feet deep. Spatters of bright red rock cling to its edges, but it's not especially remarkable. Ancient Hawaiians are said to have thrown the bones of important chiefs into it, to ensure their remains would never be disturbed. Half a mile further east, you have the additional option of cutting south across the crater, between Pu'u Naue and Pu'u Nole, to meet the Sliding Sands Trail near Kapalaoa Cabin.

The hike to Kapalaoa Cabin

If you continue east rather than heading left where the Sliding Sands Trail meets the crater floor – which you'll only have time to do if you're camping down in the crater – you enter a landscape that resembles the high mountain valleys of the western United States. The trail runs at the foot of a steep *pali*, on the edge of a delightful alpine meadow carpeted with yellow flowers, including the primitive native *moa*. Two miles along, shortly after two

successive turnoffs to the left – one is an official trail, one a "trail of use," but it's impossible to tell which is which, and in any case they soon join to cut across to the Halemau'u Trail – you come to Kapalaoa Cabin. This small, wood-frame, green-roofed cabin, on a slight mound tucked beneath the peak that's officially named Haleakalā, is the only overnight shelter in the crater that doesn't have its own campground; for details of how to make a reservation, see p.113.

The hike to Palikū Cabin

East of Kapalaoa, the Sliding Sands Trail has two more miles to run before it finally merges with the Halemau'u Trail, and the two then run together a further 1.4 miles to Palikū Cabin. The hike all the way here from the crater rim and back up again is too far to attempt in a single day; only press on if you've arranged to stay overnight. The last three miles along either trail involve a gentle descent through sparsely vegetated terrain that turns progressively greener as you approach Palikū. There are

▼ PELE'S PAINT POT

actually two cabins at Palikū, one for public use and one for the rangers; both are nestled beneath a sheer cliff, where an attractive, but generally dry, meadow gives way to a well-watered strip of forest.

Kaupō Trail

The very demanding, day-long Kaupō Trail heads south from Palikū Cabin, first through the Kaupō Gap to the edge of the park, and beyond that all the way down to meet the Pi'ilani Highway on Maui's remote south coast. It takes a couple of miles to escape the pervasive cindery dryness of the crater flow, but once past it you find you've crossed to the rain-drenched eastern side of the island.

As the walls of the Kaupō Gap rise to either side, the trail drops through dense forest, then, once out of the park, descends steeply through lush grazing land. Now that you're on Kaupō Ranch land, be scrupulous about staying on the correct trail; free-ranging bulls roam on the other side of many of the fences. After several hours of extravagant switchbacks, you finally reach the highway 200 yards east of the Kaupō Store (see p.141). Unless you've arranged to be picked up, your problems may just be beginning – little traffic passes this way.

The road to Hāna

Sculpted by rainwater cascading down the northern slopes of Haleakalā, Maui's northeast coast holds the island's most inspiring scenery. From Kahului, the Hāna Highway winds for fifty miles through this spectacular landscape to the time-forgotten hamlet of Hāna, twisting in and out of gorges, past waterfalls, and over more than fifty tiny one-lane bridges. All year, but especially in June, the route is ablaze with color from orchids, eucalyptus, and orange-blossomed tulip trees, while little fruit stands and flower stalls make tempting places to stop. Although the memorable road is not as hair-raising as legend would have it, the driving on this popular day-trip is slow going, taking around three hours each way. If you'd rather keep your eyes on the scenery than on the road, take a tour.

Hoʻokipa Beach County Park

Two miles east of Pāʻia. The best windsurfing site in Maui, if not the world, is Hoʻokipa Beach County Park. Owing to a submerged rocky ledge that starts just a few feet out, the waves here are stupendous, and so are the skills required to survive in them – this is no place for beginners. The peak season for windsurfing is summer, when the trade winds are at their most consistent. By longstanding arrangement, sailboarders can only take to the water after 11am each day. In the early morning, and on those rare winter days when the wind dies down, expert surfers flock to Hoʻokipa to ride the break known as "Pavilions" near the headland to the east.

As a beach, Hoʻokipa is not hugely attractive. It's unshaded for most of its length,

apart from a nice big grove of trees at the western end. Picnic shelters, showers, and restrooms are arrayed along a platform of lava boulders raised above the small shelf of sand. In summer, the surf can be low enough for swimming, but you still have to negotiate the seaweed-covered ledge to reach deep enough water.

So busy is Hoʻokipa that you can only approach it along a one-way loop road, which starts beyond its far eastern end; the auxiliary parking lot on the headland here is a great place from which to watch or photograph the surf action.

▼ JAWS

THE ROAD TO HĀNA

0 — 5 miles

N

ACCOMMODATION
Aloha Maui Cottages   A
Hāmoa Bay House
and Bungalow   D
Heavenly Hāna Inn   C
Huelo Point
Flower Farm   B

Jaws

Thanks to mouthwatering photo spreads in many a surfing magazine, Maui's most famous surf site these days is Jaws, a highly inaccessible spot east of Pā'ia where 70-foot waves have occasionally been recorded. Surfing there has only become at all practicable since the advent of tow-in surfing, using jet skis, in the early 1990s, and Hawaii's premier surfers now flock here in winter to do battle with monsters commonly measuring up to fifty feet. If you want to watch the action, you can reach Jaws by turning left towards the ocean five miles east of Ho'okipa, between mileposts 13 and 14 on Hwy-36; following Hanaha Road until your vehicle can take no more, which will probably be soon in an ordinary rental, and then hiking oceanwards between the pineapple fields.

The road to Huelo

Although the coastal road around East Maui is called Hāna Highway from the moment it leaves Kahului, it changes from Hwy-36 to Hwy-360 ten miles east of Pā'ia, at the foot of Hwy-365 from Makawao, and that's where you'll find mile marker 0. The first potential distraction on Hwy-360 is the unsigned turnoff, marked by a double row of mailboxes at a bend in the highway roughly 3.5 miles along, that leads down to the village of Huelo. Like many local communities, it has become an uncertain mixture of Hawaiians and wealthy *haoles*. The dirt road soon passes the plain Kaulanapueo ("resting-place of the owl") Church, built of coral cement on a black lava base and usually kept locked. It continues for a couple of miles, but neither it nor its many side roads offer access to the sea.

Not far beyond the Huelo turnoff, the picnic table immediately below the Huelo Lookout fruit stand offers an opportunity to stop and admire the views of the forest slopes and the ocean beyond.

Waikamoi Nature Trail

Just over half a mile beyond mile marker 9. The one place where you can explore the forested ridges above the Hāna Highway is along the enjoyable Waikamoi Nature Trail which sets off from an obvious roadside pull-out. This one-mile loop trail starts beyond a small picnic shelter, gently zigzagging up a muddy ridge. There are no views to speak of – it's barely possible to see beyond the tight-packed *hala* trees and green rustling bamboos hemming the track – but sunlight dapples down through the overhead canopy to magical effect. Here and

▼ WAIKAMOI NATURE TRAIL

there, you pass a variety of eucalyptus trees whose bark peels like fine tissue paper. The trail tops out at a smooth grassy clearing, with another picnic shelter, and a large mosquito population. It makes little difference whether you return by the same route, or down the adjacent jeep road that drops directly to the parking lot.

A little further along the highway, Waikamoi Falls tumbles down towards the road at a tight hairpin bend. If you want a closer look, the only place to park is immediately before the bridge – a spot it's all too easy to overshoot.

Garden of Eden Arboretum

Hwy-360, not far beyond Waikamoi Falls ☏ 808/572-9899. Daily 8am–3pm. $7.50. The small and privately owned Garden of Eden Arboretum displays an attractive assortment of native flora, including colorful orchids. It also offers a slightly distant waterfall view, and has picnic tables with a panoramic prospect of the coastline.

Honomanū Bay

Shortly after mile marker 13, the highway drops back down to sea level for the first time since Ho'okipa Beach, and you finally start to get the long coastal views for which it's famous. The Ke'anae Peninsula appears on the horizon, but much closer at hand – where the gorgeous, uninhabited Honomanū Valley, lit up by tulip trees, gives way to the ocean – you'll see the black gravel beach at Honomanū Bay. Swimming and snorkeling here is only advisable on the calmest of summer days, but it's a popular site with local surfers.

Two separate dirt tracks cut down to the shore from the

▲ KE'ANAE ARBORETUM

road as it sweeps around the narrow valley. The first, at 13.5 miles, leads down to the north shore of the stream; the second, just after mile marker 14 on the far side of the stream, is paved for the first few yards, but then becomes steeper and muddier. It comes out at the longer side of the beach.

Ke'anae Arboretum

Hwy-360, Ke'anae. Daily dawn–dusk. Free. From a wooded bend in the road a few hundred yards before mile marker 17, a paved level trail heads inland to the attractive public gardens of the Ke'anae Arboretum. Following the course of a stream you can hear but not see, it leads into a lush, narrow valley and reaches the arboretum within a quarter of a mile.

Fifty-foot-high clumps of "male bamboo" guard the entrance, with tropical plants beyond including Hawaiian species such as torch ginger and wet and dry taro. Beyond the taro fields, a mile into the park, the trail becomes a wet scramble through the rainforest, crossing up and over the valley ridge by way of tree-root footholds. Along with lots of small waterfalls, and swarms of tiny flies feasting on fallen guava and breadfruit, there's a good chance of spotting rare forest birds and even wild boar.

Ke'anae Peninsula

Not far beyond the Ke'anae Arboretum, a side road twists down to the flat Ke'anae Peninsula, the site of a small, and still predominantly Hawaiian, village. It's said that this windswept promontory consisted of bare rock until a local chief forced his followers to spend two years carrying baskets of soil down the mountainside; thereafter it became a prime taro-growing region, and supported a large population.

The taro fields are still here, surrounded by abundant banana trees and birds of paradise, and there's also a fine old church among the tall palms. The edge of the ocean is as bleak as ever, with *hala* trees propped up along the shoreline and the surf crashing onto headlands of gnarled black lava; swimming here is out of the question.

Wailua

Within a mile of Ke'anae, as the highway veers inland, the arrow-straight Wailua Road plunges down to another traditional village, Wailua. Unlike Ke'anae, its ancient rival, Wailua has always been fertile and still holds extensive taro terraces.

The lower of the two churches that stand a short way down from the turnoff is known as the Coral Miracle. Local legend has it that, in 1860, just as its builders were despairing of finding the stone to complete it, a freak storm washed up exactly enough coral on the beach below. It's a simple but attractive chapel, painted white, with turquoise stenciling around the porch and windows. Look back across the valley as you leave the building, for a superb view of the high Waikani Falls, garlanded by flowering trees at the head of the valley.

Wailua Road ends just above the tranquil mouth of Wailua Stream, which makes a sharp contrast with the ocean pummeling the beach of black pebbles beyond. Don't drive down to the stream – there's no room to turn round – and don't even consider a swim.

Wailua Valley State Wayside

Lookouts to either side of the highway beyond the Wailua turnoff offer scenic views up and down the coastline. From the inconspicuous *mauka*

▼ KE'ANAE PENINSULA

parking lot of Wailua Valley State Wayside, steps climb through a tunnel of trees to a vantage point overlooking Wailua Valley as it reaches the sea, and also inland across Keʻanae Valley, to towering waterfalls, undulating ridges, and endless trees.

Wailua Lookout

Just past mile marker 19. Beneath the Wailua Lookout, the thickly wooded gorge of Wailua Valley spreads like a little oasis, with the taller of Wailua's two churches, St Gabriel's, poking its head above the sea of trees. At the next bend, just around the corner, a big cascade roars beside the road; you have to react quickly to stop.

Puaʻakaʻa State Wayside

22.5 miles along Hāna Highway. The spacious parking lot of Puaʻakaʻa State Wayside is every bit as big as the park itself. In fact, this is a favorite stop for bus tours, because so little effort is required to negotiate the park's few yards of paved trails. If you brave the crowds, you'll see a pretty sequence of small waterfalls, with picnic tables dotted on either side of a stream.

Nāhiku

Not far after mile marker 25, a narrow unmarked road takes about three miles to wind down to the ocean. The few houses along the way constitute Nāhiku, though there's no town, just a jungle of trees and vines, some of which all but engulf the abandoned vehicles left here. The road comes out at Ōpūhano Point, from where you can look back towards Wailua atop the tree-covered cliffs reaching down into the water.

Just before mile marker 29, it's well worth stopping at the cluster of roadside shacks, centered on the *Nāhiku Fruit Stand*, which sell souvenirs, drinks, and snacks.

Kahanu Garden

ʻUlaʻino Road, Hāna ☎808/248-8912 or 332-7234, ✆www.ntbg.org. Mon–Fri 10am–2pm. $10, under-13s free. The first sign that you're finally approaching Hāna is when you pass Hāna Gardenland, a not very exciting commercial nursery, on the right. Immediately afterwards, ʻUlaʻino Road drops away to the left of Hwy-360. Three quarters of a mile down, just after the road crosses a minor ford, you'll find the entrance to Kahanu Garden, a nonprofit facility belonging to the National Tropical Botanical Garden. Over a hundred acres are devoted to tropical plants, but the land is most significant as the site of Piʻilanihale Heiau, the largest ancient *heiau* (temple) not merely in Hawaii but quite possibly in the entire Pacific. A *luakini*, or temple where human sacrifice took place, its original construction

▼ NĀHIKU

has been dated to the late thirteenth century, but it's thought to have been enlarged and rededicated by Pi'ilani around 1570 AD to celebrate his then-recent conquest

▲ PI'ILANIHALE HEIAU

of the entire island. It was rebuilt once more in the late eighteenth century, and extensively restored and reconstructed during the 1990s.

A mile-long loop trail through Kahanu Garden begins by skirting the edge of an extensive forest of splay-footed *hala* trees. A free booklet describes the traditional uses of several different species of indigenous and imported plants that have been cultivated along the way.

Your first sight of the *heiau* itself presents it towering above the lush oceanfront lawns. Constructed from black lava boulders, intricately slotted into place, and set on a natural lava flow, it's an impressive spectacle. Measuring 174 metres by 89 metres, it covers almost three acres and consists of five separate tiers on its oceanward side. As usual at such sites, however, in deference to ongoing Hawaiian religious beliefs, visitors are not allowed to set foot on the actual structure and can only admire it from a distance. As a result, you're not likely to spend more time here than the half-hour it takes to walk the trail, which also offers some gorgeous views along the coast.

The Blue Pool

'Ula'ino Road continues beyond Kahanu Garden as a rougher but still mostly paved track, almost always negotiable with care in an ordinary rental car as it undulates gently through the woods for another 1.4 miles. There are no long-range views, but it's a lovely stretch of countryside. The road ends abruptly in a shady grove a hundred yards short of the ocean, just above a stream whose outlet is blocked by a natural wall of heavy black boulders.

In recent years, the existence of a fabulous waterfall a short walk from here, popularly known as the Blue Pool, has become common knowledge among visitors to Maui. The area has therefore become rather too popular for its own good, and local residents have been infuriated by the sheer quantity of day-trippers who find their way down here. More recently, they have succumbed to the inevitable by turning their gardens into parking lots. Don't expect to park for free right at the bottom of the road, but keep going as far as you can – prices get cheaper further down, so you can expect to pay around $2 rather than the $4 on offer higher up.

To reach the shimmering Blue Pool itself, make for the shoreline, then head left for a hundred yards. Less than twenty yards from the sea, the pool is constantly replenished by water cascading from the *hala*-covered ridge above. It's set in a grotto that's festooned with ferns, vines, and *hala* trees, its mossy walls bursting with tiny pinks and peonies. As you sit on the rocks, fresh water from the falls splashes your face, while you can feel the salt spray of the ocean on your back. It's also possible to walk to the right along the beach, where coconuts lie among the boulders. Atop a spit of rough *'a'ā* lava, five minutes along, you can watch the surf crashing and grinding the black rocks to hollow out little coves, while a jungle of *hala* trees lies, unreachable, beyond.

Waiʻānapanapa State Park

Within two miles of Hāna, beyond the turnoff to Hāna Airport, a clearly signed road *makai* (oceanwards) from the highway leads through a "tunnel" of overhanging trees to the shoreline at Waiʻānapanapa State Park. To reach the main parking lot, perched above a tiny black-sand beach, turn left when you reach the park cabins at the end of the first straight stretch of road. A short and easy trail descends from the parking lot to this beautiful little cove, where the beach changes from shiny black pebbles to fine black sand as it shelves into the ocean. It looks wonderful, and barely has room to hold its daily crowd of sunbathers, but swimming is deadly, with heavy surf and deep water just a few yards out.

At the right-hand side of the beach as you face the sea, look for a hollow cave in the small cliff that you just walked down. Squeeze your way through its narrow entrance and you'll find that not only does it widen

inside, it is, in fact, a tunnel. The far end, where it's open to the ocean, is a truly magical spot.

By contrast, a very short loop trail to the left of the parking lot back at the top leads down and through Waiʻānapanapa Cave. A few yards back from the sea, this "cave" is actually a collapsed lava tube, holding two successive grotto-like pools. It's slightly stagnant and smells rather like a public restroom, but you do see some nice clinging flowers.

Coastal hiking trails in both directions make it easy to escape the throngs at the beach. Heading northwest (left), you're soon clambering over a headland of black lava through a forest of *hala* and *naupaka*. Inlets in the jagged shoreline harbor turquoise pools, while the surf rages against the rocks; in places, where the sea has hollowed out caverns, you can feel the thud of the ocean beneath you. A painting of a natural "lava bridge" here, executed in 1939 by Georgia O'Keeffe, now hangs in the Honolulu Academy of Arts. A mile or so along, the trail ends at the fence of Hāna Airport.

Southeast of the beach, the footpath crosses smoother, firmer lava, passing the park campground, a cemetery, and an impressive blowhole. After around a mile, it reaches the ruined Ohala Heiau, the walls of which remain clear despite ivy-like *naupaka* growing inside. You can continue four miles on to Hāna; the scenery is invigorating all the way, but the trail gets progressively harder to follow.

Waiʻānapanapa is by far the nicest place on Maui to camp beside the ocean (see p.160).

Hāna

For some visitors, the former sugar town of Hāna comes

PLACES The road to Hāna

as a disappointment after the splendors of the Hāna Highway. Certainly, the point of driving the road is to enjoy the scenery en route, rather than to race to Hāna itself. That said, it's pleasant enough, and remains one of the most relaxing places on Maui to spend a few days; short on swimmable beaches and golf, perhaps, but very long indeed on character, history, and beauty.

Although in ancient times Hāna controlled a densely populated region, these days it's home to just a few hundred inhabitants. Having long resisted any concept of "development" for its own sake, they proudly see themselves as one of the most staunchly traditional communities in the state.

When the local sugar plantation closed in 1943, most of its land was bought by Paul Fagan, a Californian businessman. He established not only the Hāna Ranch, whose

cowboys still work cattle herds in the fields above town, but also modern Maui's first hotel, the *Hotel Hāna-Maui*. Fagan died in 1959 – he's commemorated by a large white cross on the hillside – but the town remains dominated by the businesses he founded. Most of the town's central area is taken up by the *Hotel Hāna-Maui*, while the Hāna Ranch headquarters on the main highway houses its most conspicuous restaurant and other utilities.

Downtown Hāna

None of the buildings along the main highway, which passes through Hāna a hundred yards up from the ocean, is especially worth exploring, though Wananalua Church, whose square, solid tower contrasts appealingly with the flamboyant gardens surrounding it, makes a photogenic landmark. Across the road, the Hāna Ranch Center is a dull little mall, designed to feed and water the daily influx of bus tours, but given a flash of color by the odd *paniolo* cowboy. The original Hasegawa's General Store, stocked with every item imaginable, burned down in 1990. Since rehoused in a charmless former theater, it's still a friendly place to pick up supplies.

Hāna Cultural Center

Ua'kea Road, Hāna ☏ 808/248-8622. Daily 10am–4pm. $2 suggested donation. Local history is recalled by the low-key exhibits – gourds, calabashes, fish hooks, and crude stone idols – at the Hāna Cultural Center, down from the highway and above the bay. It also holds art exhibitions and is amassing a comprehensive collection of photos of past and present Hāna residents. A tiny nineteenth-century jail-cum-courthouse shares the same driveway, while a replica living

▲ HĀNA BAY

compound has been constructed in the grounds alongside, of the kind used by the ancient Hawaiian *maka'ainana* (common people). As well as a thatched stone dwelling and a canoe house, it features garden terraces planted with taro and *ti*.

Queen Ka'ahumanu

No figure encapsulates the paradoxes of early Hawaiian history as completely as Queen Ka'ahumanu, the daughter of Nāmāhana, a chiefess from East Maui, and Ke'eaumoku from the Big Island. Her parents' strategic alliance presented such a threat to Kahekili, the ruling chief of Maui, that they were fleeing for their lives when Ka'ahumanu was born at Hāna, around 1777.

Chief Ke'eaumoku was one of Kamehameha the Great's closest lieutenants. His daughter may have been as young as eight when she first caught the eye of the king; soon afterwards, she became the seventeenth of his 22 wives.

Ka'ahumanu was Kamehameha's favorite wife. As a high-ranking *ali'i*, she possessed great spiritual power, or *mana*. She was also an expert surfer and serial adulterer. It was after Kamehameha's death, in 1819, that she came into her own. Announcing to her son Liholiho that "we two shall rule over the land," she proclaimed herself Kuhina Nui, or Regent, and set about destroying the system of *kapus*. This elaborate system of rules denied women access to certain foods and, more importantly, to the real source of power in ancient Hawaii – the *luakini* war temples. At first Ka'ahumanu's goal was to break the grip of the priesthood, but in 1825 she converted to Christianity, after being nursed through a serious illness by Sybil Gingham, the wife of Hawaii's first missionary.

Ka'ahumanu outlived Liholiho and remained the effective ruler of Hawaii when his younger brother Kauikeaouli succeeded to the throne. After seven years spent proselytizing for her new faith, she died on June 5, 1832. Her last words were reported as "Lo, here am I, O Jesus, Grant me thy gracious smile."

Hāna Bay

Broad Hāna Bay is much the safest place to swim in East Maui, as well as being the only protected harbor in the area. The small gray-sand beach known as Hāna Beach County Park spreads to the south, at the foot of Keawa Place, backed by lawns that hold picnic tables, restrooms, and changing rooms. The park's long terraced pavilion, pressed against the curving hillside across the road, houses *Tutu's* takeout counter.

Thrusting into the ocean further south, the high cinder cone of Ka'uiki Head is the most prominent feature of the bay. Now covered with trees, it used to be just a bare rock, and served as a fortress for the ancient chiefs of Maui; Kahekili is said to have repelled an invasion from the Big Island here in 1780. Its far side – only seen easily from the air – collapsed into the sea long ago.

A short hiking trail – hard to spot at first, but soon clear enough – heads off around Ka'uiki Head from beyond the jetty, offering excellent views across the bay and up to Hāna itself. Soon after a tiny red-sand beach, it reaches a bronze plaque, set into a slab of rock near a couple of small caves in the base of the hill. This marks the birthplace of the great Hawaiian queen, Ka'ahumanu, though she was probably born later than the year it says, 1768. Continuing on, you discover that the rocky point beyond is in fact an island. Known as Pu'u Ki'i, it was once topped by a giant *ki'i* (wooden idol), erected by the Big Island chief, Umi; an automated lighthouse now stands in its place. Around the next corner, the trail is blocked by an impassable red scree slope.

Red Sand Beach

A precarious coastal footpath leads along the south flank of Ka'uiki Head to a lovely little cove that shelters one of Maui's prettiest beaches, Red Sand Beach. The Hāna Ranch, which owns the land here, considers the walk so dangerous that it makes every effort to discourage visitors; the path is often closed due to serious erosion, and should only be attempted after seeking local advice as to current conditions. To find it, walk left from the south end of Ua'kea Road, below a small, neat Japanese cemetery. Approximately a five-minute walk, the path follows, and in places spans, a narrow ledge

▼ THE TRAIL TO RED SAND BEACH

around a hillside of loose red gravel, but at this low elevation it's not too nerve-racking.

Behind a final promontory, the beach lies angled towards the rising sun, shielded by a row of black dragon's-teeth rocks, kept well flossed by the waves. Hawaiians knew this canoe landing as Kaihalulu Beach. It's only ever safe for swimming in the tiny inshore area, and even then the razor-sharp rocks beneath the surface make it essential to wear reef shoes. The origin of the beach's coarse reddish cinders – the eroded red cliffs above it – is very obvious, and it's equally obvious that you can hike no further.

Shops

Hāna Coast Gallery

Hotel Hāna-Maui, Hāna ☎808/248-8636. Probably the best array of Hawaiian arts and crafts on the island, including sculptures, turned wooden bowls and furniture, ceramics and featherwork, and plenty of paintings of East Maui landscapes.

Restaurants

Hāna Ranch

Hāna Hwy, Hāna ☎808/248-8255. Unenthralling quick-fire restaurant in the heart of Hāna, specializing in bland lunches for the daily hordes of bargain-seeking day-trippers. Mostly it's fries with everything, but a half-pound burger made from local beef costs $9.50, and they do a vegetarian taro burger, too. Dinner is served on Wednesday, Friday, and Saturday only, and is slightly more interesting; $18–33 entrees, such as barbecue ribs or

teriyaki chicken, include a salad bar. A cheaper take-out counter sells *saimin* and similar local specialties.

Hotel Hāna-Maui

Hāna Hwy, Hāna ☎808/248-8211. The deluxe resort's open-sided, wicker-furnished dining room ranks among the most expensive restaurants in Hawaii, which can make its downhome ambience and local-style service seem a little odd. Thanks to recent improvements in the kitchen, however, the food is truly superb. A real commitment to using local ingredients and techniques results in magnificent fish dishes in particular, such as *hapu* (sea bass) steamed with coconut in *ti* leaves as an entree, or a *ceviche* appetizer of *onaga* (red snapper). A changing three-course dinner menu costs $55; lunch is much simpler, centering on classy burgers and sandwiches for around $15, while breakfast is a relaxed delight.

Nāhiku Fruit Stand

Just before mile marker 29 on Hwy-360, Nāhiku. No phone. This funky, friendly roadside shack sells delicious espressos and smoothies, along with homemade lunches such as banana bread and fish specials.

Pauwela Café

375 W Kuiaha Rd, Haʻikū ☎808/575-9242. Occupying one corner of the rusting gray hulk of Pauwela Cannery, a mile off Hwy-36 and roughly five miles east of Pāʻia, this cheerful, classy neighborhood café serves delicious, inexpensive breakfasts – try the *pain perdu* (French toast) – plus salads, sandwiches, and lunch specials, all priced close to $5.

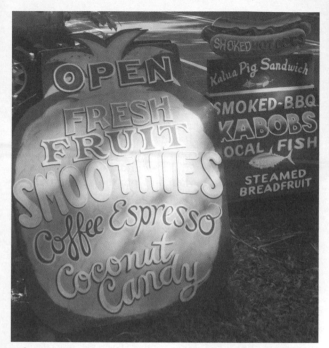

▲ NĀHIKU FRUIT STAND

Tutu's

Hāna Bay, Hāna ☎808/248-8244.
Beachfront take-out counter,
whose indifferent sandwiches,
burgers, plate lunches, sodas, and
lemonades attract long queues
every lunchtime.

Up In Smoke BBQ

Just before mile marker 29 on
Hwy-360, Nāhiku. No phone. The
perfect lunchtime snack if
you're driving the Hāna
Highway; a simple open-air
grill that serves superb $5
kebabs of smoked or fresh-
caught fish, and also baked
breadfruit.

Bars

Paniolo Lounge

Hotel Hāna-Maui, Hāna Hwy, Hāna
☎808/248-8211. This relaxed,
friendly bar provides the only
nightlife option in the whole
of East Maui. While it serves
the cocktails and snacks you
might expect, the real reason
to come is to enjoy the
performances of traditional and
contemporary Hawaiian music
by local musicians, which take
place Thursday through Sunday
evenings. Don't expect a late
night; it's all over by 9.30pm.

Beyond Hāna

Even if you only have a single day to explore East Maui, it's well worth continuing beyond Hāna. For its first few verdant miles, the scenery along Pi'ilani Highway is even more gorgeous than what came before. While the most obvious destination for day-trippers is waterfall-strewn 'Ohe'o Gulch, some great beaches lie just south of Hāna. If you're averse to returning the way you came, it's possible in normal weather to follow Pi'ilani Highway right around the whole barren coastline of southern Maui and into the upcountry above Wailea. Roughly five miles is unpaved; it's a bumpy ride, no faster than the Hāna Highway, and not as spectacular, but it does offer a glorious sense of isolation.

Kōkī Beach Park

A couple of miles south of Hāna, the Haneo'o Loop Road heads left from the highway. After half a mile, it reaches the ocean alongside the white sands of Kōkī Beach Park. Local surfers and boogie-boarders love this spot, but unless you're a very confident swimmer and all-round watersports expert, take heed of the many signs that warn of a very dangerous rip-current just offshore. It's a great place for a coastal stroll, in any case.

The exposed red cinder cone that dominates Kōkī Beach is named Ka Iwi O Pele, or "the bones of Pele," as the volcano

goddess was supposedly killed here by her sister, the goddess of the sea. Oprah Winfrey, who has purchased a number of lots in the vicinity from the Hāna Ranch, is building a home on a hundred-acre plot immediately north.

Just south of Kōkī Beach, tiny Ā'lau Islet stands just out to sea. Ancient Hawaiians re-shaped the lava rocks along the promontory closest to the island to create artificial fishponds, and fishermen are still frequent visitors.

Hāmoa Bay

1.5 miles down Haneo'o Loop Road. A couple of small roadside parking bays allow access to the grey-sand beach at Hāmoa Bay, used by *Hotel Hāna-Maui* (see p.159) for all its oceanfront activities, including a weekly *lū'au*. Once the site of a small settlement destroyed by the

▼ HĀMOA BAY

BEYOND HĀNA

Wai'ānapanapa State Park

Hāna Bay

Ka'uiki Head

Kōki Beach Park

'Ālau Island

Hāmoa Beach

'Opau Bay

Keawa Bay

HĀNA ROAD

Hāna

Wai'a'ma Bay

'Ohe'o Gulch

Ka'ū Bay

Kūhui Bay

PĪPIWAI TRAIL

Papaloa Bay

Waimoku Falls

Kīpahulu Church

Palapala Ho'omau

Lelekea Bay

KĪPAHULU VALLEY

Kalepa Pt

Mokuia Pt

Halekī'i Pt

Waiūha Bay

HALEAKALĀ

Maka'ākini Pt

NATIONAL

Kamanawai Pt

PARK

Kaupō

St Joseph's Church

Puka'auhuhu

'Apole Pt

Nu'u Bay

Pakowai Pt

We'i'opai

Kahawaihapapa

HALEAKALĀ HIGHWAY

Nakaohu Pt

Kiakeana Pt

Oma'opio

Pulehu-Waikoā

Wekea Pt

Kula

Kanaioa

Waiohuli

Keokea

POLIPOLI STATE PARK

'Ulapalakua Ranch

Tedeschi Winery

'ĀHIHI-KĪNAU NATURAL AREA RESERVE

La Pérouse Bay

Kīhei

Wailea

Mākena

Mākena Bay

Oneloa Bay (Big Beach)

'Āhihi Bay

0 5 miles

▲ 'OHE'O GULCH

tsunami of 1946, it's a good surfing spot, and holds a nice picnic area into the bargain, but it's unsafe for swimming.

The highway continues south from Hāmoa Bay through a succession of tiny residential villages, where, apart from the odd roadside fruit stand and countless crystal-clear waterfalls, there's no reason to stop.

'Ohe'o Gulch

10 miles south of Hāna. At beautiful 'Ohe'o Gulch a natural rock staircase of waterfalls descends to the oceanfront meadows at the mouth of the Kīpahulu Valley. This far-flung outpost of Haleakalā National Park, sometimes spuriously known as "Seven Sacred Pools," tends to be jam-packed in the middle of the day, but, as one of the few places on Maui to offer easy access to unspoiled Hawaiian rainforest, it shouldn't be missed. If you hike a mile or two into the hills, you'll soon escape the crowds to reach cool rock pools which, so long as it's not raining, are ideal for swimming.

Kūloa Point Trail

The paved footpath that leads downhill from the 'Ohe'o Gulch parking lot – officially, Kūloa Point Trail – is so busy

'Ohe'o Gulch practicalities

The national park at 'Ohe'o Gulch remains open 24 hours a day, and charges its standard admission fee of $10 per vehicle to all users of the roadside parking lot. That covers access to the entire park for seven days, so you only have to pay once if you visit both 'Ohe'o Gulch and the summit crater (see p.113). A ranger station just down the slope from the lot has up-to-date information on local roads and hiking trails (daily 9am–5pm; ☎808/248-7375). Guided hikes to different destinations set off daily except Saturdays at 9.30am; for details of trips on horseback in the vicinity, see p.172. Access to the upper reaches of the Kīpahulu Valley, regarded as one of the most pristine and environmentally significant regions in all Hawaii, is barred to the public. The park is, however, hoping to purchase large tracts in the valleys to the west, in order to open more hiking trails and remote beaches.

For details on camping at 'Ohe'o Gulch, see p.160.

that it's forced to operate as a one-way loop. Get here early if you want to enjoy it before the onslaught, but don't avoid it otherwise. After ambling through the meadows for five minutes, the trail winds past ancient stone walls on the low oceanfront bluff, and then down to a tiny gray-grit beach, where the shark-infested ocean is far from tempting.

However, upwards from the ocean, a "ladder" of stream-fed pools climbs the craggy rocks, an ascent negotiated by suckerfish in breeding season. Several of the pools are deep and sheltered enough for swimming, and on calm sunny days the whole place throngs with bathers. It's impossible to follow the stream as far up as the high road bridge; by then, the gorge is a slippery, narrow water chute.

Pīpīwai Trail

The Pīpīwai Trail, into the mountains above 'Ohe'o Gulch, ranks as one of the very best hikes on Hawaii (though one on which it's essential to carry mosquito repellent). Occasionally it's closed by bad weather, but the construction of two sturdy footbridges has

ensured that the first mile or so is almost always accessible. It starts beside the ranger station, but swiftly crosses the highway and heads uphill through steep fields, where thick woods line the course of the 'Ohe'o Stream.

After the first half-mile, which is by far the most demanding stretch of the hike, you come to a railed overlook facing the towering 200-foot Makahiku Falls. A little further up, a deep groove in the earth heads right, leading to a series of shallow bathing pools just above the lip of the falls, where the stream emerges from a tunnel in the rock. As well as commanding magnificent views, it's an utterly idyllic spot for a swim on rain-free days.

Continuing along the main trail, you immediately pass through a gate in a fence, to emerge into an open guava orchard where you'll soon hear the thundering of smaller waterfalls to your right. There's no way to get to the water, but you'll see it framed through the thick jungle, together with the gaping cave mouth it has hollowed out on the far side. A little further on, you may be lured off the trail again by a pair of twin falls near a small concrete dam, which can be admired from a rocky outcrop in the streambed below.

Beyond that lies a lovely meadow, with views to the high valley walls in the distance, laced by huge waterfalls. A mile up, the trail crosses high above the stream over the newly built bridges and then follows a dark and narrow gap through a forest of huge old bamboo interspersed with sections of level wooden boardwalk. Eventually, two miles up from the road, you'll spot the

▲ KAUPŌ STORE

spindle-thin, 400-foot Waimoku Falls ahead. Reaching its base requires a lot of scrambling, and close to the end you have to cross the stream itself on stepping stones. Despite the obvious danger of falling rocks, many hikers choose to cool off by standing directly beneath the cascade. Allow a good two hours to complete the entire round-trip hike.

Kīpahulu

Within a mile of 'Ohe'o Gulch, the highway passes through the village of Kīpahulu. Time seems to have stood still in this attractive little spot since the local sugar mill closed down eighty years ago. The only sign of life these days comes from the occasional lunchtime fruit stand selling the produce of the roadside orchards.

Palapala Ho'omau Church

A quarter-mile beyond milepost 41 at Kīpahulu, a paved road branches left off the highway.

After a couple of hundred yards, turn left again onto a dirt road through a "tunnel" of trees, and park by the giant banyan tree at the end that guards the Palapala Ho'omau Church. Founded in 1864, it has whitewashed coral walls and a green timber roof, and is set in pretty clifftop gardens. The interior is utterly plain and unadorned.

Visitors make their way to this tranquil spot because the fenced-off platform of black lava stones in the churchyard holds the grave of Charles Lindbergh (1902–74), who won fame in 1927 as the first man to fly across the Atlantic and later achieved notoriety as a Nazi sympathizer. Lindbergh retired to Maui late in life, and died within a couple of years. Leading off from the cemetery, and only accessible through it, Kīpahulu Point Park is a small, shaded lawn, fringed with bright orange-leafed bushes, where the picnic tables command wonderful ocean views.

Along the South Maui coast: the Pi'ilani Highway

It takes roughly an hour and twenty minutes to drive along the Pi'ilani Highway from Kīpahulu to the Tedeschi

Driving the Pi'ilani Highway

For many years, the rangers at 'Ohe'o Gulch were forbidden to recommend that visitors drive all the way around southern Maui on the Pi'ilani Highway, but only very rarely these days are they obliged by flooding to declare it formally closed. At any rate, check at the ranger station for advice on the road's current condition before setting out. All the rental car companies forbid clients to come this way, but that's more because it's inaccessible if you need emergency help than because it's especially difficult. It is, however, best not to drive this route after dark.

Kahikinui

The southern shoreline of Maui used to be known as Kahikinui, or Tahiti Nui; the equivalent part of Tahiti, which has the same outline as Maui, bears the same name. Archeologists treasure it as one of the very few areas where Hawaii's modern population is so small that ancient habitation patterns and structures can still be readily discerned. They've dated several *heiaus* (temples) and other remains as having been constructed around the start of the seventeenth century, a time when it's thought Maui had just been united under a single ruler, Pi'ilani himself, for the first time.

Winery in Upcountry Maui, and a minimum of two hours to reach Kahului. Thus it saves little if any time to return this way rather than back along the Hāna Highway. On the other hand, it will show you, literally, another side of the island, and one that still looks much as it did before outsiders ever reached Hawaii.

The countryside immediately beyond Kīpahulu is lovely, dotted with exclusive homes whose owners are no doubt happy that this is not yet a standard tourist loop. After less than two miles, Pi'ilani Highway returns to sea level – for the first time in several miles – and skirts the long gray-pebble beach at Lelekea Bay. As you climb the cliffs at the far end, look back to see water spouting out of the hillside above an overhang in the rock, forceful enough to be a gushing jet rather than a waterfall.

The pavement gives out after the second of the two little coves that follow. An overlook 2.3 juddering miles further on looks down on the small, flat promontory holding the 1859 Huialoha Church. A mile after that, the solitary Kaupō Store is an atmospheric general store that's normally open on weekdays only.

By now, the landscape has become much drier, and you're starting to get views up to the

Kaupō Gap, where a vast torrent of lava appears to have petrified as it poured over the smooth lip of Haleakalā Crater. To the east, you can peek into the lushness of the upper Kīpahulu Valley, but the slopes to the west are all but barren.

Beyond St Joseph's Church, which stands below the highway a mile beyond the Kaupō Store, the pavement starts up again and the road begins to mount the long southern flank of Haleakalā at the gentlest of angles. There's no tree cover on the deeply furrowed hillside – where some of the cracks seem like incipient Waimea Canyons – so cattle gather beneath the occasional shade tree beside the road.

Naked russet cinder cones lie scattered to either side of the road, some bearing the traces of ancient Hawaiian stone walls, while rivers of rough black *'a'ā* lava snake down to the sea. An especially vast hollow cone, near the 20-mile marker, marks the spot where small huts and ranch buildings start to reappear. Soon Mākena becomes visible below, with Molokini and Lanai out to sea, and three miles on it's a relief to find yourself back in green woodlands. The Tedeschi Winery (see p.109) is a little over a mile further on, with another 23 miles to go before Kahului.

Lanai

The island of Lanai, nine miles west of Maui, measures just thirteen miles by eight. Thanks partly to its mysterious allure as a so-called "private island," it's a popular day-trip by ferry from Maui. Don't picture Lanai as the ultimate unspoiled Hawaiian island, however; it largely lacks the lush scenery and sandy beaches of its neighbors. Indeed, until the twentieth century, ancient Hawaiians and modern settlers alike barely bothered with this dry and barren mound of red dirt; then began its seventy-year reign as the world's largest pineapple producer. These days, Lanai belongs almost entirely to billionaire David Murdock, who has shut down the plantation and redeveloped Lanai as an exclusive resort. The former plantation village of Lāna'i City is the site of all the island's hotels and restaurants, except for the *Manele Bay Hotel*, on the south coast near Lanai's only swimming beach.

Mānele Bay

Ferries from Maui to Lanai arrive at Mānele Bay, on the south coast eight miles from Lāna'i City. As parched and barren as a Greek island, the bay is protected from the open ocean by the high flat-faced cliff on its eastern side, which glows red when it's hit by the setting sun. People fish from the rocks or picnic nearby, and the odd brave soul dodges the boats to go snorkeling, but there's nothing much here apart from an overpriced little snack bar, the *Harbor Cafe*.

▼ MĀNELE BAY

Visiting Lanai

Scheduled flights serve tiny Lanai Airport, four miles southwest of Lāna'i City, from both Kahului on Maui and from Honolulu. For travelers based on Maui, however, the best way to reach Lanai is on the *Expeditions* ferry (☎808/661-3756 or 1-800/695-2624, ⊛www.go-lanai.com; $25 each way, under-12s $20). It sails from Lahaina to Mānele Bay daily at 6.45am, 9.15am, 12.45pm, 3.15pm, and 5.45pm, while departures from Lanai are at 8am, 10.30am, 2pm, 4.30pm, and 6.45pm. The trip takes approximately 50 minutes.

The harbor is a very short walk from Hulupo'e Beach, the island's best, but shuttle buses also meet each arriving ferry at the harbor. They charge a $5 flat fare, whether you're going up to Lāna'i City or just taking the 500-yard hop to the *Mānele Bay Hotel*.

Map labels:

LANAI

ACCOMMODATION	
Hotel Lanai	A
Lanai Plantation Home	B
Lodge at Kō'ele	C
Mānele Bay Hotel	D

Polihua Beach · Shipwreck · Shipwreck Beach · Shipwreck · Pō'aiwa Petroglyphs · Keanapapa Point · Garden of the Gods · KĀNEPU'U FOREST PRESERVE · POLIHUA RD · POLIHUA TRAIL · KA'ENA TRAIL · Maunalei Gulch · Ho'okio Gulch · Hauola Gulch · Kō'ele · Keōmuku · Lāna'i City · MUNRO TRAIL · Lāna'ihale 3370 · Makaīwa Point · Lōpā · KAUMALAPAU HWY · MĀNELE RD · PĀLĀWAI BASIN · Pōka'i · Kaumalapau Harbor · Lāna'i Airport · KAUPILI RD · Naha · Kaunolū · Mānele Bay · Hulopo'e Bay · N

0 Miles 3

PLACES Lanai

Hulopo'e Beach

Only accessible by road from Mānele Bay, but also reached via a footpath down from the *Mānele Bay Hotel* (see p.160), curving, sandy Hulopo'e Beach is by far the best swimming beach on Lanai.

The only facility for hotel guests at the beach is a small equipment kiosk at the west end. Its main users tend to be local families rather than tourists, who come to swim, picnic, and explore the tidepools at the foot of Mānele Cone, the extinct cinder cone that divides Hulopo'e Bay from Mānele Bay. The snorkeling here can be excellent, especially in the morning, while the offshore waters are among the best diving sites in Hawaii. Regular dive trips are organized by Trilogy Ocean Sports (☏808/565-7700 ext 2387 or

☏1-888/225-6284, ⓦwww .sailtrilogy.com).

The black lava walls of an ancient Hawaiian village are clearly visible between the hotel and the beach. Sometimes it held permanent residents, who grew gourds and sweet potatoes, while during other periods it served as a seasonal fishing camp. Signs

▼ HULOPO'E BEACH

Exploring Lanai

Lanai has the most rudimentary road system imaginable, with less than thirty miles of paved highway, none of which runs along the coast. For visitors, the only significant stretches are the eight-mile Mānele Road from Lāna'i City down to Mānele Bay, and the four miles of Kaumalapau Highway between Lāna'i City and the airport. Free shuttle buses ferry guests at the three hotels along these routes; anyone who's using the restaurants, or simply looks confident, should have no problem hopping a ride.

The only way to explore the island in any depth is by renting a four-wheel-drive vehicle from Lāna'i City Service in Lāna'i City (daily 7am–7pm; ☎808/565-7779 or 1-800/JEEP-808). A basic Wrangler Jeep costs around $130 per day; be warned that you're liable for any damage, which can easily amount to several thousand dollars for a basic mishap in the sand.

In addition, the Adventure Lanai Ecocenter (☎808/565-7373, ⊛www.adventurelanai .com) organize jeep tours, which involve some hiking, at $100 for a half-day trip, and also kayaking, downhill biking, and hiking excursions. *The Lodge at Kō'ele* rents out mountain bikes for $40 per day, and runs horseback expeditions.

explain how the whole place used to look.

As detailed on p.160, it's possible to camp at Hulopo'e Beach.

The Pālāwai Basin

As you head up from the coast to Lāna'i City, it's easy to drive through the Pālāwai Basin, at the top of hill, without realizing that it's the collapsed caldera of the volcano that built Lanai. The entire 15,000-acre basin – until just a few years ago, the largest pineapple field on earth

– is a bowl-shaped depression. The high mountain ridge on its eastern side stands thousands of feet taller than the low rise to the west, while the bowl spills over altogether to flow down to the ocean on the southern side. Nothing is planted now in the fields, but the occasional vivid flowering tree lights up the highway.

Lāna'i City

To think of Lāna'i City as a town requires a stretch of the imagination; for it to call itself

▼ PĀLĀWAI BASIN

▲ LĀNA'I CITY

a "city" is little short of absurd. This neat, pretty community of just 2500 people was laid out on a basic grid in 1924 to house laborers from the plantations, and it has barely changed since. You have to search to find a two-story building: the leafy backstreets hold rows of simple cottages, identical but for the colors they're painted and the flowers in their gardens.

Virtually all the daily business of Lanai revolves around Dole Park. The main road, Lāna'i Avenue, runs along the eastern end, while over a hundred ninety-foot Cook Island pines rise from the wiry grassland in the center, towering over the stores, cafés, and offices that line all four sides.

The Munro Trail

The only way to explore the mountainous ridge that forms Lanai's "backbone" is along the ill-defined Munro Trail, a twelve-mile loop trip from Lāna'i City that's much easier to drive (in a 4WD vehicle) than it is to walk. This rutted track starts from the main road just north of *The Lodge at Kō'ele*, and climbs through a forest of towering Cook Island and Norfolk Island pines to the 3370-foot summit of Lāna'ihale.

On clear days, that's the only spot in Hawaii from which it's possible to see five other islands.

Shipwreck Beach

On island maps, Keōmuku Road, which runs the full length of Lanai's east coast, might appear to offer plentiful beaches, sleepy long-lost towns, and ocean views. In reality it's a long, hard drive for very little reward, and you're better off simply driving its paved section as far as the sea, where drivers with 4WD vehicles can take a short detour north to Shipwreck Beach.

That name is informally applied to the whole of Lanai's northern shoreline, thanks to its remarkable history of maritime accidents. Countless vessels have come to grief in these shallow, treacherous waters; the coast is littered with fragments, while two large wrecks remain stuck fast a few hundred yards offshore. Some historians even believe that a sixteenth-century Spanish galleon was wrecked somewhere along here, long before Captain Cook reached Hawaii.

The sand road that leads to Shipwreck Beach peters out roughly 1.5 miles from the point where Keōmuku Road reaches the ocean. Walk in the same direction for a few yards, as far as a ruined lighthouse, to see the rusting orange hulk of a World War II "Liberty Ship" propped up on the rocks, almost completely out of the water.

Walking two hundred yards inland from here brings you to

PLACES Lanai

a gulch where boulders still bear petroglyphs carved by ancient Hawaiians, including tiny stick drawings and bird-headed figures.

Garden of the Gods

Three miles northwest of Lāna'i City. Lanai's most famous scenic spot is reached by a *very* dirty jeep drive across the red dust bowl of the central plateau. The extraordinary Garden of the Gods looks more like the "badlands" of the Wild West than anything you'd expect to find in Hawaii. This small desert wilderness is predominantly a rich russet red, but its unearthly hillocks and boulders are scored through with layers of lithified sand of every conceivable hue – grays, yellows, ochres, browns, and even blues. At sunset, the whole place seems to glow, and the rocks lying scattered across the red sands cast long, eerie shadows.

Countless rock cairns are stacked everywhere you look. Ranging from meticulous piles of boulders, diminishing in size, to precarious towers of pebbles, it's easy to imagine them as relics of a bygone age. They're not; they owe their existence to a craze that swept Hawaii in the 1980s, when locals erected stone "shrines" in isolated places in the misguided belief that it was an ancient Hawaiian tradition.

Cafés

Café 565

408 Eighth St, Lāna'i City ☎808/565-6622. As well as pizzas and calzones, this small café, with open-air seating alongside Dole Park, serves sandwiches, plate lunches, and even sushi.

Coffee Works

604 Ilima St, Lāna'i City ☎808/565-6962. Spacious coffee bar a block north of Dole Park, behind the post office. Besides the espressos, they also sell a few cheap sandwiches, smoothies, and ice cream, which you can enjoy on the large *lāna'i*.

Pele's Other Garden

Eighth St and Houston, Lāna'i City ☎808/565-9628. Closed Sun. Bustling health-food deli, with juices and wholesome $7 sandwiches to take out or eat in at lunchtime, and more formal entrees in the evening, such as a gnocchi pasta special for around $17.

Restaurants

Blue Ginger Café

409 Seventh St, Lāna'i City ☎808/565-6363. Closed weekends. Simple café-restaurant alongside Dole Park. It's a favorite local rendezvous, though the food is just basic plate lunches and pizzas, all for about $8.

Canoes Lanai

419 Seventh St, Lāna'i City ☎808/565-6537. A local-style diner, complete with swivel stools and soda fountain, serving burgers, *saimin* (noodle soup), and big fry-ups for breakfast and lunch only.

Formal Dining Room

The Lodge at Kō'ele, Lāna'i City ☎808/565-4580. Extremely formal restaurant, with a lofty reputation and silver-service treatment; male diners must wear jackets. Reserve early and savor the presentation as much as the food, which is a richer, meatier version of the usual upscale Hawaiian resort cuisine.

Typical appetizers include carpaccio of venison and foie gras, both priced at just under $20; entrees, upwards of $42, include rack of lamb, steak, and seafood; and there are some amazing chocolate desserts.

Henry Clay's Rotisserie

Hotel Lanai, 828 Lāna'i Ave, Lāna'i City ☎808/565-7211. Friendly, intimate dining room, open for dinner only, but with an adjoining bar that remains open late each night. Under the keen supervision of its New Orleans–born chef/manager, the Cajun-influenced menu makes full use of local ingredients, with entrees ranging all the way from pizza ($16) to local venison ($38). Almost anything you choose, from an oyster in a shot glass ($1.35), to an appetizer of mussels in saffron broth ($10), to a fish entree ($25), is likely to be excellent.

Hulopo'e Court

Mānele Bay Hotel ☎808/565-7700. The less formal of the oceanfront hotel's two restaurants, the lovely, breezy *Hulopo'e Court* opens for breakfast and dinner only, charging $24 (full) or $16 (continental) for the morning buffet, and around $34 for delicious evening menu items such as steamed *moi* (threadfish).

Ihilani Dining Room

Mānele Bay Hotel ☎808/565-7700. The dinner-only *Ihilani Dining Room* serves "Mediterranean Gourmet" cuisine, with steamed and grilled island fish or roast meat for around $40, and five-course set menus at $85 ($125 with wine) per person.

The Terrace

The Lodge at Kō'ele, Lāna'i City ☎808/565-4580. Marginally the less formal of *The Lodge's* two restaurants, with indoor and outdoor seating overlooking the lawns, the *Terrace* serves generally health-conscious food, but still at quite high prices: even an egg-and-ham breakfast costs $12. Lunch is the best value, with $8 fresh-made soups and $13 grilled meat and fish dishes. Typical dinner entrees include slow-roasted lamb shank on couscous, and roasted chicken (both $28).

▼ HULOPO'E COURT

Accommodation

Hotels, resorts, and B&Bs

Maui is small enough to be easily explored from a single base; only if you'd like to spend time in the rainforests of East Maui is it worth planning a two-center vacation. Most of the island's accommodation options are concentrated close to its finest beaches in two highly developed coastal strips: between Lahaina and Kapalua on the lush leeward shoreline of West Maui, or in what's known as South Maui, between Kīhei and Mākena on the drier and less scenic, but more central, southwest shoreline of the eastern half of the island. The most luxurious resorts of all are in Wailea in the south and Kā'anapali in the west, but there are cheaper alternatives nearby.

Travelers looking for a secluded paradise-island hideaway should consider the little B&Bs tucked away in Upcountry Maui and around Hāna. If you're not driving, Lahaina is the only place where you can stay in a real town with sightseeing, beaches, and restaurants within easy walking distance. For budget travelers, the cheapest options of all are in faded downtown Wailuku.

For a reliable selection of top-quality B&Bs, contact Hawaii's Best Bed & Breakfasts (☎808/985-7488 or 1-800/262-9912, ⊛www.bestbnb.com).

Lahaina

See the map on p.52 for locations of these listings.

Best Western Pioneer Inn 658 Wharf St ☎808/661-3636 or 1-800/457-5457, ⊛www.pioneerinnmaui.com. Historic, highly atmospheric hotel on the seafront in the very center of Lahaina. The tastefully furnished rooms, all with private bath and a/c, open onto a lovely *lānai* overlooking Banyan Tree Square, and there are also some luxurious two-bedroom suites. There's a small pool, but no on-site parking. Rooms cost $125–170, while suites are $170–190.

Lahaina Inn 127 Lahainaluna Rd ☎808/661-0577 or 1-800/669-3444, ⊛www.lahainainn.com. Sumptuous, antique-furnished re-creation of how a century-old inn ought to look, set slightly back from Front Street above the *Lahaina Grill* (see p.58). The twelve rooms of varying sizes have a/c, private bathrooms (most with showers rather than baths) and phones, but no TV. No children under 15 years. Rates range from $125 to 175.

Lahaina Shores Beach Resort 475 Front St ☎808/661-3339 or 1-800/642-6284, ⊛www.lahainashores.com. Large, airy shorefront hotel facing a pretty little beach a few hundred yards south of central Lahaina, next door to the 505 Front Street mall. Two-person rooms cost around $190, three- and

---

While the average cost of a single night's accommodation is currently around $190 in high season, you can still expect to find a good hotel, condo, or B&B for more like $100. In theory, room rates are at their highest from Christmas to Easter, and from June to August – but don't expect to save more than perhaps $15–20 per night in a typical hotel by visiting in low season. The rates quoted here, unless otherwise indicated, are for the cheapest double room in high season. All room rates are subject to an additional state tax of 11.25 percent.

Condo rentals

Many of Maui's hotels double as condo properties, where individual owners also let out their apartments through various specialist agencies. In addition, the agencies themselves often handle other privately owned vacation rentals, including oceanfront villas.

The agencies listed below offer a wide range of properties, generally at prices starting around $100 per night in low season, rising to $130 between Christmas and March. Be sure to check whether there's an additional one-time "cleaning fee," which is usually around $50.

Kīhei

Condominium Rentals Hawaii 362 Huku Li'i Place, #204, Kīhei, HI 96753 ☎808/879-2778, 1-800/367-5242 (US) or 1-800/663-2101 (Canada), ☻www.crhmaui.com

Kīhei Maui Vacations PO Box 1055, Kīhei, HI 96753 ☎808/879-7581 or 1-888/568-6284 (US & Canada), ☻www.kmvmaui.com

Maui Condominium and Home Realty 2511 S Kīhei Rd, Suite H, PO Box 18400, Kīhei, HI 96753

☎808/879-5445 or 1-800/822-4409 (US & Canada), ☻www.vacationweb.com/mchr

Māʻalaea

Māʻalaea Bay Rentals ☎808/244-7012 or 1-800/367-6084, ☻www.maalaeabay.com

Pāʻia

Maui Vacation Properties ☎808/575-9228 or 1-800/782-6105, ☻www.maui.cc

four-person suites from $250; all have kitchens and *lānais*; an ocean view costs around $30 more than a mountain view. **Ohana Maui Islander** 660 Waineʻe St ☎808/667-9766 or 1-800/462-6262, ☻www.ohanamauiislander.com. The *Outrigger* chain operates this low-key but attractively furnished and good-value complex a couple of blocks from the sea in central Lahaina. The 360 accommodation options range from hotel rooms costing from $109 to two-bedroom condos starting at $159, in several separate buildings connected by a rambling system of walkways through colorful gardens. There's also a swimming pool and tennis courts.
Old Lahaina House PO Box 10355 ☎808/667-4663 or 1-800/847-0761, ☻www.oldlahaina.com. Good-quality B&B accommodation in a friendly private home with pool, a few hundred yards south of downtown Lahaina. There's one guest room in the house and four more in a separate garden wing; all are en-suite, with refrigerators, TVs, and a/c. Rates include breakfast on the *lānai*; rooms start at $69, suites at $150.

Plantation Inn 174 Lahainaluna Rd ☎808/667-9225 or 1-800/433-6815, ☻www.theplantationinn.com. Luxury B&B hotel, not far back from the sea and styled after a Southern plantation home, complete with columns and verandahs and a twelve-foot-deep pool. All 19 rooms have bathrooms and *lānais*; prices start at $160, while the suites, which also have kitchenettes, cost $225–250. Guests get a discount at the downstairs restaurant, *Gerard's* (see p.59).

Kāʻanapali

See the map on p.64 for locations of these listings.
Hyatt Regency Maui 200 Nohea Kai Drive ☎808/661-1234 or 1-800/554-9288, ☻www.maui.hyatt.com. Kāʻanapali's grandest hotel, with opulent gardens, a palm-filled atrium with a pool of live penguins, and a vast labyrinth of swimming pools including a swinging rope bridge and bar. A ten-story main tower and subsidiary wings house a total of 800-plus luxurious rooms, four restaurants including

the sumptuous *Swan Court* (see p.64), and a full-service oceanfront spa; a nightly *lū'au* is held alongside (see p.65). Mountain-view rooms start at $345; expect to pay upwards of $450 for an ocean view.

Kā'anapali Beach Hotel 2525 Kā'anapali Parkway ☎808/661-0011 or 1-800/262-8450, ✉www.kbhmaui.com. The least expensive option on Kā'anapali Beach, located between Whaler's Village and the Black Rock. This low-rise property, arrayed around attractive oceanfront lawns, has a fine stretch of beach plus a whale-shaped swimming pool complete with *tiki* bar. All of its large, well-equipped rooms have balconies or patios, though some offer shower rather than bath. An especially strong commitment to preserving Hawaiian culture is reflected in regular classes and performances. Garden views from $200, ocean views from $275.

Maui Eldorado Resort 2661 Keka'a Drive ☎808/661-0021 or 1-888/339-8585, ✉www.mauieldorado.com. Condo property consisting of several low buildings ranged up the hillside, well back from the shoreline; shuttle buses run to the resort's private beachfront area. All units offer a/c, *lānai*, maid service, washer/dryer, and a kitchenette or full kitchen; typical prices range from $159 to $275.

Maui Marriott Resort and Ocean Club 100 Nohea Kai Drive ☎808/667-1200, 1-800/763-1333, ✉www.marriott.com. Imposing, luxurious resort hotel at the south end of Kā'anapali Beach, offering extra-large rooms, two swimming pools with a water slide and a pirate lagoon for kids, twenty on-site shops, three restaurants (including a beachside restaurant and an espresso bar), a nightly *lū'au*, exercise facilities, and good-value room-and-car package deals. Garden-view rooms start at $309, while an ocean view will cost around $50 extra.

Royal Lahaina Resort 2780 Keka'a Drive ☎808/661-3611 or 1-800/280-8155, ✉www.2maui.com. One of Kā'anapali's two original resorts, commanding a long strip of perfect sand at the north end of the beach; it's slightly showing its age, but then it's significantly cheaper than its neighbors, especially if you book online. The hotel has 600 rooms, with a central 12-story tower of plush suites costing $180–395, another

smaller hotel building with rooms at $149–189, and a couple of dozen "cottages" of condo-style apartments on the grounds, priced upwards from $250. Amenities include two upscale restaurants, a nightly *lū'au*, and a 3500-seat tennis stadium that's occasionally used for concerts.

Sheraton Maui Resort 2605 Kā'anapali Parkway ☎808/661-0031 or 1-888/488-3535, ✉www.starwoodhawaii.com /sm.cfm. This large luxury resort was the first to open at Kā'anapali, in 1963, and has since been almost entirely rebuilt, with five tiers of rooms dropping down the crag of Black Rock and separate oceanfront wings, plus a lovely pool and lagoon, all at the broadest end of Kā'anapali Beach. Garden-view rooms start at $350, while for an ocean view you'll pay at least $425.

The Westin Maui 2365 Kā'anapali Parkway ☎808/667-2525, ✉www .westinmaui.com. High-rise hotel in the center of Kā'anapali Beach, immediately south of Whaler's Village, where the five swimming pools are fed by artificial waterfalls and feature some great waterslides, and there's a lagoon of live flamingos to match the predominantly pink decor. Not surprisingly, it's a major favorite for families with young children. Bright, modern, luxurious hotel rooms, all with private *lānai*; prices range upwards from $339 for a garden view, $405 for an ocean view.

The Whaler on Kā'anapali Beach 2481 Kā'anapali Parkway ☎808/661-4861 or 1-800/367-7052, ✉www.the-whaler .com. Just north of Whaler's Village, this condo resort holds comfortable one- and two-bedroom units, each with lavish bathroom, *lānai*, and full kitchen. Most of the rooms don't face the ocean, and cost from $181 – those that do cost little extra, starting at $201 – but all the accommodation itself is good, and there's also a small pool.

Northwest Maui

See the map on p.67 for locations of these listings.

Aston Kā'anapali Shores 3445 Lower Honoapi'ilani Rd, Honokōwai ☎808/667-2211 or ☎1-877/997-6667, ✉www .kaanapalishores.com. Grand oceanfront condo development, right on the beach at the south end of Honokōwai, with two nice pools and a/c throughout. Typical rooms start at $155, while the large family suites are good value, costing from $207. Tennis is free, but parking costs $9 per night. Book online for the best rates.

Aston at Papakea Resort 3543 Lower Honoapi'ilani Rd, Honokōwai ☎808/669-4848 or ☎1-877/997-6667, ⊛www .astonhotels.com. Oceanfront Honokōwai complex of condo suites of all sizes, priced from $155 for the smallest or $184 for a larger option. They're housed in eleven buildings arranged around two matching gardens, each of which has a pool, spa, lagoon, and putting course.

Embassy Vacation Resort 104 Kā'anapali Shores Place, Honokōwai ☎808/661-2000 or 1-800/669-3155, ⊛www.embassyvacationresorts.com. Giant pink ziggurat at the south end of Honokōwai, right on the ocean just beyond Kā'anapali Beach, and complete with a one-acre pool, a 24ft waterslide, and a 12th-floor rooftop miniature golf course. Prices for the one- and two-bedroom units start at $325; all have separate living rooms, shower and bath facilities, kitchenettes, and all are large enough to accommodate at least five guests. A free buffet breakfast is prepared daily.

Hale Maui 3711 Lower Honoapi'ilani Rd, Honokōwai ☎808/669-6312, ⊛www .maui.net/~halemaui. Small family-run "apartment hotel" in Honokōwai, offering one-bedroom suites from just $85. They sleep up to five guests, with kitchens, washer-dryers, and *lānais*, but there's limited maid service.

Kahana Reef 4471 Lower Honoapi'ilani Rd, Kahana ☎808/669-6491, 1-800/451-5008, ⊛www.mauicondo.com. Four-story row of well-furnished – if characterless – studios and one-bedroom units, right next to the sea, though there's little beach here. The rates are relatively low, starting at $140, but there's no a/c. Discounted car rental available.

Kahana Sunset 4909 Lower Honoapi'ilani Rd, Kahana ☎808/669-8011 or 1-800/669-1488, ⊛www .kahanasunset.com. Luxury condos, spacious inside but squeezed close together, in lush gardens by a lovely sandy beach that's

effectively restricted to guests only. Garden-view rates range $135–210; only the larger two-bedroom units, which cost $220–390, enjoy ocean views.

Kahana Village 4531 Lower Honoapi'ilani Rd, Kahana ☎808/669-5111 or 1-800/824-3065, ⊛www.kahanavillage .com. Large and very comfortable two- and three-bedroom condos, right beside the ocean if not a beach. The views are great, and the rooms good value for small groups, costing from $205, but the pool is small and the loft-like second bedrooms in the upper-level apartments can seem like an afterthought. Five-night minimum stay.

Kapalua Bay Hotel 1 Bay Drive, Kapalua ☎808/669-5656 or 1-800/367-8000 (US & Canada), ⊛www.kapaluabayhotel.com. This gorgeous luxury resort was closed for restoration as this book went to press. It's likely to reopen even better than before, so check the website for the latest news.

The Mauian 5441 Lower Honoapi'ilani Rd, Nāpili ☎808/669-6205 or 1-800/367-5034 (US & Canada), ⊛www .mauian.com. Very friendly, laid-back little resort, in vintage 1950s architectural style, facing ravishing Nāpili Beach and consisting of three two-story rows of tastefully furnished studio apartments with kitchenettes. Those nearest the ocean start at $130; further back you'll pay around $25 less. The only phone and TV is in the communal lounge and library, which is also where the complementary breakfast is served.

Nāpili Bay Resort 33 Hui Drive, Nāpili; reserve through Maui Beachfront Rentals ☎808/661-3500 or 1-888/661-7200, ⊛www.mauibeachfront.com/napili/bay .html. Small, fairly basic individually owned studio apartments for $125, in a superb oceanfront location on Nāpili Beach. Each has a kitchenette and *lānai*, and is capable of sleeping four guests.

Noelani 4095 Lower Honoapi'ilani Rd, Kahana ☎808/669-8374 or 1-800/367-6030 (US & Canada), ⊛www.noelani -condo-resort.com. Fifty condo apartments of all sizes, set on a promontory, so all units enjoy views across to Molokai. Prices start at $130; pluses include cable TV and VCR, plus use of two oceanfront pools, a Jacuzzi, and laundry facilities.

Outrigger Royal Kahana 4365 Lower Honoapi'ilani Rd, Kahana ☎808/669-5911 or 1-800/447-7787 (US & Canada), ⊛www.outrigger.com. This oceanfront condo building, standing twelve stories high in central Kahana, enjoys views of Molokai and Lanai. While it's less intimate than the family resorts of Nāpili, it's undeniably smart, and all the a/c units, which include studios as well as one- and two-bedroom suites, have kitchens, washer-dryers, and private *lānais*. Garden-view rooms start at $129, ocean views at $145.

Polynesian Shores 3975 Lower Honoapi'ilani Rd, Kahana ☎808/669-6065 or 1-800/433-6284, ☎808/669-0909. Friendly, fifty-room condo property, with shared pool, oceanfront lawns, and good snorkeling. Units of all sizes are available, all with kitchens and *lānais*, from $130.

Ritz-Carlton, Kapalua 1 Ritz-Carlton Drive, Kapalua ☎808/669-6200 or 1-800/262-8440, ⊛www.ritzcarlton .com. The sheer elegance of this opulent, marble-fitted *Ritz-Carlton* can make it feel a bit formal for Maui, but there's no disputing the level of comfort, with three swimming pools, a nine-hole putting green to complement the three nearby golf courses, ten tennis courts, spa, and croquet lawn. See p.71 for details of the regular Tuesday-evening slack key guitar concerts. Prices start at $380.

Kahului

See the map on pp.72–73 for locations of these listings.

Maui Beach Hotel 170 W Ka'ahumanu Ave ☎808/877-0051 or 1-888/649-3222; or reserve through Castle Resorts ☎808/591-2235, 1-800/367-5004 (US & Canada) or 1-800/272-5275 (HI), ⊛www .castleresorts.com. Faded seafront hotel offering 150 run-down rooms from just $105, plus free airport shuttles. Available through the same lobby are cheaper, even less appealing rooms in the unattractive *Maui Palms* next door, which is only partly operational.

Maui Seaside Hotel 100 W Ka'ahumanu Ave ☎808/877-3311 or 1-800/560-5552 (US & Canada), ⊛www.mauiseasidehotel .com. Bland but reasonably well-kept waterfront hotel, with a swimming pool and its own artificial beach. The location, across from the shopping malls, is hardly romantic, but at least it is by the sea, and the *Seaside* makes a convenient and relatively inexpensive base. Rooms that face inland start at $90, ocean-view ones at $125; for the best rates, book online.

Wailuku

See the map on p.78 for locations of these listings.

Banana Bungalow 310 N Market St ☎808/244-5090 or 1-800/846-7835, ⊛www.mauihostel.com. Friendly unofficial hostel, open to non-Hawaiian residents only, in a run-down light-industrial area not far from central Wailuku. Beds in two- and three-bed dorms cost $20, while basic private rooms are from $40 single, $50 double. Guests can hang out in the gardens and living rooms. There's one free shuttle daily to the airport and to Kanahā beach, plus a changing rotation of free excursions to all parts of the island. The hostel also offers free Internet access and use of a Jacuzzi.

Northshore Hostel 2080 Vineyard St ☎808/986-8095 or 1-866/946-7835, ⊛www.northshorehostel.com. Recently refurbished budget accommodation in downtown Wailuku, with communal kitchen facilities. Beds in plain, four- and six-bed dorms cost $25, or $20 with leaflets available at the airport, while equally plain private rooms – each with just a bed or two bunks, and a closet – go for $50 single, $60 double. A more comfortable private double with en-suite half-bath costs $70. Seventh night free. Popular with European travelers, who leave their surfboards propped against the giant banyan in the courtyard. The hostel offers free beach shuttles and bus trips to different parts of the island, and also plan to open a part-Indian, part-vegetarian restaurant downstairs, *Bohemian Plaza*.

Old Wailuku Inn at Ulupono 2199 Kaho'okele St ☎808/244-5897 or 1-800/305-4899, ⊛www.mauiinn.com. A spacious plantation-style home, set in landscaped gardens a short walk south of central Wailuku, that's been converted into a luxurious ten-room B&B. All rooms have tasteful 1930s-era furnishings, attractive Hawaiian quilts, private *lānais* and baths, and are equipped with VCRs; some also have whirlpool spas. The upstairs rooms enjoy good views. Guests share use of a living room and verandah, and eat a generous breakfast communally. Price range $125–180; two-night minimum stay.

Central Maui

See the map on p.83 for the location of this listing.

The Inn at Mama's Fish House 799 Poho Place, Pā'ia ☏808/579-9764 or 1-800/860-4852, ⊛www.mamasfishhouse.com. Six fully equipped, tropically styled rental apartments right beside Kuau Beach, and alongside a popular restaurant. Three have two bedrooms and look out over the ocean, and cost $475; the others have one, but can still hold four guests. They're set slightly back in lush gardens, and cost $175.

Kīhei

See the map on p.92 for locations of these listings.

Aloha Pualani Hotel Boutique 15 Wailana Place ☏808/875-6990 or 1-866/870-6990 (US & Canada), ⊛www.alohapualani.com. Five two-story suites across from Mā'alaea Bay at the north end of Kīhei, recently overhauled to provide luxurious personalized accommodations which start at $235. Each has a living room, kitchen, bedroom, and *lānai*, and they're clustered around a central pool and bar. On-site owners provide breakfast and advice. Two-night minimum stay.

Hale Kai O'Kīhei 1310 Uluniu Rd ☏808/879-2757 or 1-800/457-7014 (US & Canada), ⊛www.maui.net/~hkok; also available through Condominium Rentals Hawaii (see box, p.152). Three stories of straightforward one- and two-bedroom condos, costing from $110, in an absolutely stunning and very quiet beachfront location, near Kīhei's best malls and restaurants.

There's also a private coconut grove, spacious *lānais*, and discounted car rental.
Kama'ole Nalu Resort 2450 S Kīhei Rd ☏808/879-1006 or 1-800/767-1497, ⊛www.kamaolenalu.com. Large beachfront complex set on neat lawns at the south end of Kama'ole Park 2. Two-bedroom, two-bath condos, all with kitchen and laundry facilities; the long, private *lānais* provide spectacular sunset views. Garden-view rooms start at $135, ocean views at $155. Five-night minimum stay, and discounts on car rental.

Kīhei Akahi 2531 S Kīhei Rd; available through Condominium Rentals Hawaii ☏808/879-2778, 1-800/367-5242 (US) or 1-800/663-2101 (Canada), ⊛www.crhmaui.com. The ascending rows of good-value, well-furnished condos (all capable of sleeping four) in this garden property across from Kama'ole Park 2 have use of two swimming pools and a tennis court, but no views to speak of. Rates start at $85; four-night minimum stay.
Mana Kai Maui 2960 S Kīhei Rd; available through Condominium Rentals Hawaii ☏808/879-2778, 1-800/367-5242 (US) or 1-800/663-2101 (Canada), ⊛www.crhmaui.com. Large building beside lovely Keawakapu Beach at the grander south end of Kīhei, with small hotel rooms starting at $90 and full-blown condo apartments from $160, plus a pool and the excellent *Five Palms* grill restaurant (see p.95).
Maui Coast Hotel 2259 S Kīhei Rd ☏808/874-6284, 1-800/663-1144 or 1-800/895-6284 (US & Canada), ⊛www.mauicoasthotel.com. Tasteful, luxurious, and good-value modern hotel, set slightly back from the highway opposite Kama'ole Park 1. Standard hotel rooms from $165, as well as pricier one- and two-bedroom suites, with good deals on car rental, plus an attractive pool with poolside bar, and an above-average restaurant, *Spices*.
Maui Vista 2191 S Kīhei Rd ☏808/879-7966; reserve through Marc Resorts ☏808/922-9700 or 1-800/535-0085 (US & Canada), ⊛www.marcresorts.com. Comfortable, well-equipped condos of all sizes, from $150 per night, on the hillside across from Kama'ole Park 1. Not the best

views, but amenities include three pools and six tennis courts.

Royal Mauian Resort 2430 S Kīhei Rd ☎808/879-1263 or 1-800/367-8009 (US & Canada), ✆www.royalmauianresort .com. Huge, luxurious, oceanfront condo complex, though lacking a/c, beyond the south end of Kamaʻole Park 1. Highlights include the lovely views, especially from the roof terrace, and a nice pool. Rates start at $175; five-night minimum stay, and discounts on car rental.

Sunseeker Resort 551 S Kīhei Rd ☎808/879-1261 or 1-800/532-6284 (US & Canada), ✆www.mauisunseeker.com. This pretty little hotel-cum-condo building, which caters to a predominantly gay clientele and offers a hair salon and massage, stands very close to Māʻalaea Bay beach (and, unfortunately, also the main road) at the north end of Kīhei. As renovated by its enthusiastic owners, it offers great-value rooms and suites from $115, all with kitchen facilities and ocean views. Guests enjoy free access to the hot tub and deck at the adjoining *Wailana Inn*. Three-night minimum stay.

Wailana Inn 14 Wailana Place ☎808/874-3131 or 1-800/399-3885 (US & Canada), ✆www.wailanabeach .com. The ten lovingly retro-furnished rooms in this twin-story block, resembling an old-fashioned motel and set just back from the main road in northern Kīhei, are much nicer than the exterior might suggest. All are spacious and comfortable, and include kitchens or kitchenettes, plus TV and phone, while guests share use of a rooftop hot tub and sundeck; prices start at $145. As with the neighboring *Sunseeker*, most of the guests are gay, though straight visitors are very welcome.

Wailea and Mākena

See the map on p.98 for locations of these listings.

Fairmont Kea Lani Maui 4100 Wailea Alanui Drive ☎808/875-4100 or 1-800/441-1414, ✆www.fairmont.com. Locals call it the Taj Mahal, but this dazzling white resort is more like something from the *Arabian Nights*. Despite its flamboyant

domed silhouette, the interior is characterized by smooth unadorned curves, and you can see through the lobby to lily ponds and the lagoon-cum-pool, crossed by little footbridges. Two huge wings of plush rooms (all equipped with TVs and DVD players), 37 garden villas, and some excellent restaurants are all focused on lovely Polo Beach (see p.97); there's also a great Italian deli. Rates start at $350 for a garden view, $450 for an ocean view.

Four Seasons Resort Maui at Wailea 3900 Wailea Alanui Drive ☎808/874-8000 or 1-800/334-6284, ✆www .fourseasons.com. Lavish resort property at the south end of Wailea, with a large, beautiful, white-sand beach on view beyond the open lobby, and a gorgeous, palm-ringed pool. Rooms have private *lānais*, bamboo furnishings, and 24-hour room service, and you can choose from several restaurants, including *Spago* (see p.104). Mountain-view rooms cost from $350, garden-view or ocean-view rooms or suites from $450.

Grand Wailea Resort 3850 Wailea Alanui Drive ☎808/875-1234 or 1-800/888-6100, ✆www.grandwailea.com. Large and very ostentatious resort hotel, with a five-level swimming pool ("Wailea Canyon") that's linked by waterslides and features a swim-up bar, hot-tub grottoes, and even a water elevator back to the top. There's also a luxurious spa, half a dozen restaurants, a nightclub, and tropical flowers everywhere. The published rack rates start at $475 for a terrace view, $810 for an ocean view, but you can normally find discounts of around thirty percent online.

Maui Prince 5400 Mākena Alanui Drive ☎808/874-1111 or 1-866/774-6236, ✆www.mauiprince.com. South Maui's southernmost resort is a secluded and stylish low-rise facing gorgeous, sandy Maluaka Beach, and just about within walking distance of the even more wonderful Big Beach (see p.99). The main hotel block focuses inwards around a central courtyard; the rooms are spacious, pared-down, and elegant, with prices starting at $335; and there are trickling ponds filled with *koi* carp everywhere you look. Top-quality Japanese and Pacific Rim restaurants, golf packages,

pilates, and yoga on the beach, and early-morning snorkel cruises to nearby Molokini. Look for great room-and-car deals online.
Outrigger Palms at Wailea 3700 Wailea Alanui Drive ☎808/879-1922 or 1-888/294-7731 (US & Canada), ⊛www .outrigger.com. Though Wailea's first resort hotel has been thoroughly upgraded to match its neighbors, it retains its original open-air appeal. Comprised of several small buildings in landscaped gardens and a larger central tower, all with spacious, comfortable rooms, the hotel offers three pools, two restaurants, plus Hawaiiana lectures and four weekly *lū'aus* (see p.166). The nearest beach is, however, ten minutes' walk away. Garden-view rooms start at $209, ocean-view ones at $225.
Renaissance Wailea Beach Resort 3550 Wailea Alanui Drive ☎808/879-4900 or 1-800/992-4532, ⊛www .renaissancehotels.com. A highly luxurious resort, stacked in seven tiers above twin crescent beaches and boasting swimming pools set amid lush gardens. Almost 350 sumptuous rooms come with VCRs and *lānais* angled towards the ocean. Those closest to the sea start at $399, while mountain views cost from $309. There's also a thrice-weekly *lū'au*.

Upcountry Maui

See the map on p.106 for locations of these listings.
Hale Ho'okipa 32 Pakani Place, Makawao ☎808/572-6698, ⊛www .maui-bed-and-breakfast.com. Tucked away on a quiet residential street, this lovely timber-built plantation-style home abounds in tasteful architectural detail. Its three well-furnished en-suite B&B rooms share a common living room and cost $95–165, where good breakfasts are served in a friendly atmosphere. There's also a cottage for rent in the grounds, for $145.
Kili's Cottage; reserve through Hawaii's Best B&B, PO Box 758, Volcano, HI 96785 ☎808/985-7488 or 1-800/262-9912, ⊛www.bestbnb.com. A real bargain: a comfortable three-bedroom, two-bathroom house, set in beautiful upland gardens below Pūlehu, equipped with TV, VCR, and

full kitchen, and rented for $115, less than the price of most Maui hotel rooms. Two-night minimum stay.
Kula Lodge RR1 ☎808/878-1535 or 1-800/233-1535, ⊛www.kulalodge .com. Upmarket board and lodging in a Hawaiian approximation of an Alpine inn, *makai* of Haleakalā Highway, just before the Haleakalā Crater Road turnoff. Accommodation is in five chalets, four of which can sleep family parties: all are comfortably furnished, though they don't have phones or TV, and cost $115–175.
Malu Manu 446 Cooke Rd ☎808/878-6111 or 1-888/878-6161, ⊛www.maui .net/~alive/. Two short-term rentals in seven acres of gardens, enjoying magnificent views, 4000 feet up the flanks of Haleakalā. Besides a fully furnished two-bedroom house costing $185, there's a smaller "writer's retreat" cabin for $150; both are furnished with antiques and share use of an outdoor hot tub. Three-night minimum stay.
Pilialoha 2512 Kaupakalua Rd, Ha'ikū ☎808/572-1440, ⊛www.pilialoha .com. Small cottage in the gardens of a private home above Ha'ikū, with kitchen, bathroom, and space enough to sleep four comfortably. $130 per night, three-night minimum stay.

The road to Hāna

See the map on p.124 for locations of these listings.
Aloha Maui Cottages PO Box 790210, Pā'ia ☎808/572-0298, ⊛www .alohamauicottages.com. Very rural B&B, not far off Hwy-360 thirteen miles east of Pā'ia, consisting of four simple but attractive and comfortable cabins that cost $60–135. The cheapest, which share a bathroom, are a bargain for budget travelers. The helpful owner can lend you a bike, but you'll need a car to get here. Three-night minimum.
Hāmoa Bay House and Bungalow PO Box 773, Hāna, HI 96713 ☎808/248-7884, ⊛www.hamoabay.com. Two fabulous rental properties, splendidly isolated – even from each other – two miles south of Hāna. The bungalow rents for $195;

perched on stilts in a jungle-like setting, and with an open-air Jacuzzi on its wooden *lānai*, it makes an idyllic honeymoon hideaway. The house is large enough for two couples, and costs $250. Both have Balinese bamboo furnishings, and require a three-night minimum stay.

Heavenly Hāna Inn PO Box 790, Hāna Hwy ☎808/248-8442, ◉www .heavenlyhanainn.com. Exquisite Japanese-style B&B, set in rolling fruit gardens beside the highway two miles north of central Hāna, and holding three gorgeous suites, priced at $190–260, plus a large common living area, where Japanese food is among the breakfast options. Two-night minimum stay.

Huelo Point Flower Farm PO Box 791808, Pā'ia ☎808/572-1850, ◉www .mauiflowerfarm.com. Luxury clifftop accommodation thirteen miles east of Pā'ia, with spectacular views over Waipi'o Bay, plus an on-site waterfall and open-air waterfront Jacuzzi. Two separate cottages at $150 and $200 – the cheaper Gazebo Cottage still makes a lavish, private honeymoon retreat – plus larger houses appropriate for four or six guests, costing $350–450.

Hāna

See the map on p.131 for locations of these listings.

Hāna Kai-Maui Resort 1533 Ua'kea Rd ☎808/248-8426 or 1-800/346-2772 (US), ◉www.hanakaimaui.com. Small, eighteen-unit condo set in lovely multi-level gardens overlooking Hāna Bay, a short way north of Hāna Beach County Park. Each well-equipped studio and one-bedroom unit has a kitchen and private *lānai*; the larger ones sleep four. Studios for $125–145 with apartments costing between $145–195; fifth night free.

Hotel Hāna-Maui 5031 Hāna Hwy ☎808/248-8211 or 1-800/321-4262,

◉www.hotelhanamaui.com. Secluded luxury hotel, built in the 1940s as Hawaii's first self-contained resort and integrated into the community to create a unique atmosphere. In addition to the older rooms in the Bay Cottages near the lobby, which start at $395, rows of plantation-style Sea Ranch cottages are arranged across the lawns that drop down to the ocean. They have no TVs, but boast every other creature comfort, with kitchenettes and private *lānais* that have individual hot tubs and enjoy great views; prices range up to $895, the closer you get to the sea. As well as regular shuttles to Hāmoa Beach for activities, hotel guests have use of tennis courts and a pitch-and-putt golf course, and there's regular live music in the lounge.

Joe's Place PO Box 746, 4870 Ua'kea Rd ☎808/248-7033, ◉www.joesrentals .com. Joe himself passed away some years ago, but his ordinary Hāna home, opposite the *Hāna-Kai Maui Resort*, still offers eight simple rooms, sharing a kitchen and communal lounge. All cost $45 except the one that has its own en-suite bath, priced at $55; there are no sea views, but this is Hāna's best option for budget travelers.

Lanai

See the map on p.143 for locations of these listings.

Hotel Lanai 828 Lāna'i Ave ☎808/565-7211 or 1-877/665-2624, ◉www .hotellanai.com. Appealing bungalow hotel, perched at the edge of the woods above Dole Park. Built for Jim Dole in the 1920s, it's now run by an enthusiastic young management team who have spruced it up into an inexpensive, low-key alternative to the resorts. Guests nonetheless have free access to the resort facilities (except the pool at the *Mānele Bay Hotel*) and can make use of the same free bus services. Accommodation is in ten simple en-suite

---

Cottages in and around Hāna

Hāna Ali'i Holidays (☎808/248-7742 or 1-800/548-0478, ◉www.hanamauitravel .com) offers the choice of some twenty apartments and cottages in and around Hāna, many by the ocean, and some absolutely gorgeous. Rates range from $80 to $450 a night, but $110–150 should get you a spacious and attractive cottage.

Camping

Opportunities to camp on Maui are very limited, with the best sites being in Haleakalā National Park, in and near the crater, as detailed on p.113, and also at Kīpahulu on the southeast shore, where there's a free and extremely rudimentary first-come, first-served oceanfront campground at 'Ohe'o Gulch.

There's also great oceanfront camping at Wai'ānapanapa State Park, where tent camping costs $5 per person, while basic cabins, each holding up to four people, cost $45 per cabin. Permits are available from the Department of Land and Natural Resources, 54 S High St, Wailuku, HI 96793 (Mon–Fri 8am–3.30pm; ☎808/984-8109, ⊛www.state.hi.us/dlnr), but the cabins are usually reserved far in advance.

On Lanai, you can camp for up to a week at Hulopo'e Beach's tiny, peaceful six-pitch campground (☎808/565-3982). There's a charge of $5 per person per night, plus a one-time $5 registration fee.

rooms at $105–135, or a self-contained cottage for $175.

Lanai Plantation Home 547 Twelfth St ☎808/565-6961 or 1-800/566-6961 (Hawaii), ⊛www.dreamscometruelanai .com. This restored plantation home, set in nice gardens a short walk southeast of Dole Park, has four very comfortable guest rooms, each with a luxurious en-suite bathroom, that can be rented out individually at $98.50, or as part of the entire house, costing $380.

The Lodge at Kō'ele PO Box 310, Lāna'i City, HI 96763 ☎808/565-7300 or 1-800/450-3754, ⊛www .islandoflanai.com. Quite why The Lodge should win the Condé Nast Traveler readers' poll as the world's best tropical resort is anyone's guess, since the gorgeous, immensely luxurious hotel is several miles from the ocean, 1600ft up in a pine forest reminiscent of the Scottish Highlands. The ambience is pure country-house, and most of the one hundred rooms – tucked away in the low bungalows around the "executive putting course" and croquet lawns – are comfortably furnished rather than opulent. Guests have full privileges and beach access at the Mānele Bay

Hotel. Rooms cost anything from $400 up to $2200.

Mānele Bay Hotel Lāna'i City 96763; ☎808/565-7700 or 1-800/450-3754, ⊛www.islandoflanai.com. Despite its name, the Mānele Bay Hotel is not actually at Mānele Bay, although its jade-tiled roof is visible from the harbor. It spreads itself instead across the hillside above the much nicer Hulopo'e Beach, a few hundred yards west. Although The Lodge at Kō'ele is regarded as the island's flagship hotel, the Mānele Bay conforms far more closely to what most visitors want from Hawaii: a lovely beach, ocean views, marble terraces, cocktails by the pool, and plenty of sun. Its 250 lavishly appointed rooms (some of which come with their own private butler) are arranged in two-story terraced buildings, engulfed by colorful gardens, with a golf course alongside. The whole property has a very strong Chinese theme, with antique bronzes and vases, and centers on a wonderful pool. There's also a luxury spa, where Hawaiian treatments such as lomi lomi massage or ti-leaf wraps ($100 and up for 45min) are available. Terrace-view rooms cost $400, garden- or ocean-view rooms between $525–3500.

Essentials

Arrival

All flights to **Maui** from beyond Hawaii, and the vast majority of flights from the other Hawaiian islands, land at **Kahului Airport**, a couple of miles east of Kahului on the central isthmus. All the national rental car chains are represented at the airport, and while there are no scheduled bus services, it is possible to catch a shuttle bus to wherever you're staying, with either Aloha Tours (☎ 808/879-2828, ✆ www.akinatours.com) or Speedishuttle (☎ 808/661-6667 or 1-800/977-2605, ✆ www.speedishuttle.com). Typical rates start at around $25 per person to Kīhei, $35 to Lahaina, and $50 to Nāpili. Taxis are also available.

In addition, **Kapalua** in West Maui, which is much closer to the resorts of Kā'anapali and Lahaina, receives around six daily flights from Honolulu, while local commuter services also land at tiny Hāna airport in East Maui.

Though plans are afoot to introduce high-speed ferries to Maui from Honolulu, currently the island's only ferries connect Lahaina with Lanai and Molokai; see p.142.

Information

The best source of visitor information on Maui is the local "chapter," as it's called, of the **Hawaii Visitors Bureau** (☎ 808/244-3530 or 1-800/525-MAUI, ✆ www.visitmaui.com). You can order a copy of their glossy guide-cum-directory to the island through their website, though in truth it consists largely of advertisements. Their main office on the island itself, tucked away half a mile northeast of central Wailuku at 1727 Wili Pa Loop (Mon–Fri 8am–4.30pm), stocks plenty more printed material.

In West Maui, the Lahaina Visitor Center, inside the Old Lahaina Court House on Banyan Tree Square (daily 9am–5pm; ☎ 808/667-9193 or 1-888/310-1117, ✆ www.visitlahaina.com), stocks a smaller array of brochures and leaflets.

You'll find websites for accommodation, activities, and all kinds of other things listed throughout this guide. Otherwise, the most useful site for Maui as a whole is ✆ www.maui.net, an all-purpose Maui portal which features links to accommodation agencies, individual properties, activities, and local newspapers like the *Maui News* and *Haleakala Times*.

Transportation

It's virtually impossible to make the most of a Maui vacation without renting your own vehicle, but the island does offer a rudimentary public transport network.

Driving on Maui

In the absence of adequate roads to cope with its volume of tourists, the traffic on Maui is consistently bad. The worst areas are the woefully inadequate Mokulele Highway between Kīhei and Kahului, and the narrow Honoapiʻilani Highway around West Maui, where drivers habitually make sudden stops in winter to watch whales in the ocean. At least the snail's pace along the Haleakalā and Hāna highways is owing to the natural obstacles en route, and gives you a chance to appreciate the scenery. Rental companies forbid their clients to drive off-road, which can lead to trouble if you're heading for obscure beaches or surf sites. In the past, those strictures have applied to both the Kahekili Highway in West Maui, and the remote Piʻilani Highway along the southern coast of East Maui, but they seldom do so any longer.

All the national **rental car chains** are represented at Kahului Airport and at or near Kapalua Airport; in addition, Avis has branches in Kīhei, Wailea, and Kapalua; Budget has an office in Wailea; and Dollar is in Hāna. Local alternatives include Wheels R Us, which rents cars, motorcycles, and mopeds, and accepts drivers under age 25, at three locations: 741 Wainee St in Lahaina (☎808/667-7751), 2439 S Kīhei Rd in Kīhei (☎ 808/875-1221), and 75 Kaʻahumanu Ave, Kahului (☎808/871-6858).

Buses

Maui's bus network is operated by Holo Kaʻa Public Transit (☎ 808/879-2828, ⊛ www.akinatours.com). They run five daily **buses** between Wailea and Kāʻanapali, via Kīhei, Māʻalaea, and Lahaina; two between Kīhei and Kapalua via Lahaina; and buses from Wailuku and Kahului (but not the airport) to Māʻalaea, where you can connect with the other routes. They also offer frequent connec-

tions between Lahaina and Kāʻanapali, and between Kīhei and Wailea.

In addition, the West Maui Shopping Express (☎808/566-7420 or 1-800/533-8765) operates two bus routes in the Lahaina area, both connecting the Wharf Cinema Center mall with the Whaler's Village mall in Kāʻanapali; one calls at all the major hotels in Kāʻanapali, the other connects the two malls with the Lahaina and Puʻukoliʻi train stations. The similar South Maui Shopping Express (☎ 808/566-7420 or 1-800/533-8765) operates a regular shuttle between Mākena and Māʻalaea, via Wailea and Kīhei, from 5.50am until 10pm daily.

Cycling

Among companies renting out **mountain bikes**, typically at $25–30 per day or up to $120 per week, are South Maui Bicycles, 1993 S Kīhei Rd, Kīhei (☎ 808/874-0068); West Maui Cycles, 1087 Limahana Place, Lahaina (☎ 808/661-9005, ⊛ www.westmauicycles.com); and Island Biker, 415 Dairy Rd, Kahului (☎808/877-7744, ⊛www.maui.net/~rjn). Chris' Bike Adventures (☎ 808/871-2453) can arrange customized **bike tours** of Maui to your specifications. A full list of operators running **downhill bike rides** on Haleakalā appears on p.172.

Ferries

Lahaina Harbor is home to the only scheduled **inter-island ferry services** in Hawaii. Ferries sail from in front of the *Pioneer Inn* to Mānele Bay on **Lanai** five times daily and return from there as often; see the box on p.142 for complete information on this service.

Money

Although it's possible to have an inexpensive vacation on Maui, there's no getting away from the fact that prices in Hawaii are consistently higher than in the rest of the US. How much you spend each day is, of course, up to you, but it's hard to get any sort of breakfast for under $8, a cheap lunch can easily come to $15, and an evening meal in a restaurant, with drinks, is likely to cost $30 or more per person, even if you're trying to economize.

As outlined in the Accommodation chapter, Maui has a couple of hostels (in Wailuku), which charge around $20 for a dorm bed, but otherwise even the cheapest hotels and B&Bs tend to charge well over $80 a night for a double room, and a rental car with gas won't cost less than $30 a day. It's easy to spend $100 per person per day before you've done anything: pay for a snorkel cruise, let alone a helicopter ride, and you've cleared $140.

A state **sales tax** of 4.166 percent is imposed on all transactions. Hotels tack on an additional 7.25 percent tax, adding a total of 11.42 percent to accommodation bills.

Most visitors find that there's no reason to carry large amounts of cash or travelers' checks to Hawaii. **ATMs**, which accept most cards issued by domestic and foreign banks, can be found almost everywhere; call your own bank if you're in any doubt. The two major **banks** are the Bank of Hawaii, which belongs to the Plus network of ATMs, and the First Hawaiian Bank, which belongs to the Plus and Cirrus networks. Even the smallest town tends to hold a branch of one or the other.

If you do want to take **travelers' checks** – which offer the great security of knowing that lost or stolen checks will be replaced – be sure to get them issued in US dollars. Foreign currency, whether cash or travelers' checks, can be hard to exchange, so foreign travelers should change some of their money into dollars at home.

For most services, it's taken for granted that you'll be paying with a credit card. Hotels and car rental companies routinely require an imprint of your card whether or not you intend to use it to pay.

Food and drink

Gone are the days when the Hawaiian islands were self-sufficient Gardens of Eden; the state now produces less than twenty percent of the food it consumes, and in many ways eating in Maui can be much like eating anywhere else in the US.

However, two important factors work in favor of visitors hoping for memorable culinary experiences. First of all, there's the island's ethnic diversity. Immigrants from all over the world have brought their own national dishes and recipes to Hawaii, and those separate traditions have repeatedly mingled to create intriguing new cuisines. Second, the presence of thousands of tourists, many prepared to pay top rates for good food, means that the island holds some truly superb fine-dining restaurants, run by internationally renowned chefs.

Note that all restaurants are now obliged by law to forbid smoking.

Local restaurants

Maui has its fair share of outlets of the national fast-food chains, but locally owned budget restaurants, diners, and take-out stands serve a hybrid cuisine that draws on the traditions of Japan, China, Korea, and the Philippines, as well as the US mainland. The resultant mixture has a slight but definite Hawaiian twist. In fact, the term "local" food has a distinct meaning in Hawaii, and specifically applies to this multicultural melange.

Breakfast tends to be the standard combination of eggs, meat, pancakes, muffins, or toast. At midday, the usual dish is the plate lunch, a molded tray holding meat and rice as well as potato or macaroni salad and costing from $6 to $9; *bento* is the Japanese equivalent, with mixed meats and rice, while in Filipino diners you'll be offered *adobo*, pork or chicken stewed with garlic and vinegar. Korean barbecue, *kal bi* – prepared with sesame – is especially tasty, while *saimin* (pronounced *sy-min*), a bowl of clear soup filled with noodles and other ingredients, has become something of a national dish. Finally, the carbohydrate-packed *loco moco* is a fried egg served on a hamburger with gravy and rice.

Food in general is often referred to as *kaukau*, and it's also worth knowing that *pupus* (pronounced *poo-poos*) is a general term for little snacks, the kind of finger food that is given away in early-evening happy hours.

Lū'aus

These days, there's no such thing as an authentic "Hawaiian" restaurant; the closest you can come to eating traditional foods is at a **lū'au**. Primarily tourist money-spinners, and always accompanied by pseudo-Polynesian entertainment, these offer the chance to sample such dishes as *kālua* pork, an entire pig wrapped in *ti* leaves and baked all day in an underground oven; *poke*, which is raw fish, shellfish, or octopus, marinated with soy and oriental seasonings; *poi*, a purple-gray paste produced by pounding the root of the taro plant; and *lomi-lomi*, a dish made with raw salmon. As *lū'aus* always involve mass catering and canteen-style self-service, the food itself, with the exception of

Lahaina's *The Feast at Lele*, is not sufficient incentive to go.

Below is a round-up of the main *lū'aus* on offer on the island.

Drums of the Pacific, *Hyatt Regency Maui*, Kā'anapali ☏808/661-1234. Daily. $79. See p.65.

The Feast at Lele, 505 Front St, Lahaina ☏808/667-5353, ⊛www.feastatlele.com. Daily. $99. See p.59.

Maui Sunset Lū'au, *Maui Prince*, Mākena ☏808/875-5888. Tues, Thurs & Sat. $72. See p.104.

Marriott Lū'au, *Maui Marriott*, Kā'anapali ☏808/661-5828. Daily. $80.

Old Lahaina Lū'au, Lahaina Cannery Mall, Lahaina ☏808/667-1998, ⊛www .oldlahainaluau.com. Daily. $85. See p.61.

Royal Lahaina Lū'au, *Royal Lahaina Resort*, Kā'anapali ☏808/661-9119, ⊛www.lahainaluau.com. Daily. $77.

Wailea's Finest Lū'au, *Outrigger Palms at Wailea*, Wailea ☏808/879-1922. Mon, Tues, Thurs & Fri 5pm. $72.

Fine dining

Many of Maui's best **restaurants** are in its most expensive hotels, and a meal in the showcase resorts of Kā'anapali and Wailea can cost as much as $100 per head. However, less exclusive communities such as Lahaina, Kīhei, and Pā'ia all manage to support a wide range of excellent eating options at more affordable prices. In the last few years, a distinctive Hawaiian cuisine has begun to emerge, known variously as **Pacific Rim**, **Euro-Asian**, or **Hawaii Regional**. In its ideal form it consists of combining foods and techniques from all the countries and ethnic groups that have figured in Hawaiian history, using the freshest ingredients possible. Top chefs, like Roy Yamaguchi of *Roy's*, preserve natural flavors by flash-frying meat and fish like the Chinese, baking it whole like the Hawaiians or even serving it raw like the Japanese. The effect is enhanced with Thai herbs and spices, and by the inventiveness of modern Californian cooking.

Maui also has plenty of conventional **American** shrimp and steak specialists, as well as high-class **Italian**, **Thai**, and **Chinese** places. Many restaurants offer all-you-can-eat **buffets** one or more nights of the week; they all sacrifice quality to quantity, so you might as well go for the cheaper ones. Lastly, to cater for that much-prized customer, the Japanese big-spender, some large hotels have very good Japanese restaurants.

Drink

The usual range of **wines** (mostly Californian, though Maui does have its own Tedeschi Winery; see p.109) and beers is sold at Maui restaurants and bars. At some point, however, every visitor seems to insist on getting wiped out by a **tropical cocktail** or two. Among the most popular are the Mai Tai, which should contain at least two kinds of rum, together with orange Curaçao and lemon juice; the Blue Hawaii, in which vodka is colored with blue Curaçao; and the Planter's Punch, made with light rum, grenadine, bitters, and lemon juice.

Tap water is safe to drink. If you're hiking, however, never drink untreated stream water.

Tours

Bus tours

The most popular **bus tours** on the island run around East Maui to Hāna (typically costing $80–100 per person), and up the volcano to Haleakalā Crater (more like $70–80). Operators include Akina Aloha Tours (☎808/879-2828, ✆www .akinatours.com), Polynesian Adventure Tours (☎808/877-4242 or 1-800/622-3011, ✆ www.polyad.com), and Ekahi Tours (☎808/877-9775 or 1-888/292-2422, ✆www.ekahi.com).

Flight-seeing tours

Helicopter **flight-seeing tours** are firmly established as a must-do activity for any visitor to Hawaii. A full round-island flight over Maui, which will enable you to see such wonders as Haleakalā Crater and the summit of the West Maui mountains from above, takes more than an hour and costs around $200. If you'd prefer a shorter flight, try a 20- or 30-minute loop over West Maui.

For discounted rates, buy tickets through an activities operator such as Tom Barefoot's, as detailed on p.172. Target prices are $75 for a 20-minute jaunt, something over $150 to fly over Haleakalā and Hāna, and more than $200 to fly over to nearby Molokai or Lanai as well. Visibility is almost always best in the early morning.

It's also possible to take an airplane or "fixed-wing" tour, with Volcano Air Tours

---

Helicopter tour companies

The helicopter companies listed below run tours from Kahului Airport; none currently operates from Kapalua. Blue Hawaiian, which uses the ultra-quiet ECO-Star helicopters, are particularly recommended.

Air Maui ☎808/877-7005 or 1-877/238-4942, ✆www.airmaui.com
Alexair Helicopters ☎808/871-0792 or 1-888/418-8458, ✆www.helitour .com
Blue Hawaiian Helicopters ☎808/871-8844 or 1-800/745-2583, ✆www.bluehawaiian.com

MauiScape ☎808/877-7272 or 1-888/440-7272, ✆www.mauiscape.net
Sunshine Helicopters ☎808/871-5600 or 1-800/469-3000, ✆www .sunshinehelicopters.com

Ocean sports

ESSENTIALS

(☎808/877-5500, ✪www.volcanoairtours .com), which flies across to the active volcano on the Big Island from Kapalua or Kahului for around $300.

The Sugar Cane Train

The **Sugar Cane Train** ($18.95 round-trip, under-13s $12.95; ☎808/667-6851 or, in the US only, 1-800/499-2307, ✪www.sugarcanetrain.com) is a restored locomotive (complete with "singing conductor") that runs six-mile, half-hour excursions through the cane fields along the tracks of the old Lahaina & Kā'anapali

Railroad. It travels from Lahaina to Kā'anapali and then half a mile beyond to turn around at Pu'ukoli'i. For anyone other than a small child, it's not exactly an exciting trip. The first departure from Lahaina is at 11.05am daily and the last at 4pm; from Kā'anapali, the first is at 10.25am daily, the last at 3.10pm. There's also a weekly dinner train, setting off from Pu'ukoli'i at 5pm on Thursday (adults $76, under-13s $43). Free shuttle buses connect the Lahaina and Kā'anapali stations with the Wharf Cinema Center and the Whaler's Village, respectively.

Ocean sports

With average water temperatures of between 75°F and 82°F (24–28°C), the sea in Maui is ideal for **ocean sports**. These range from snorkeling and scuba

diving to fishing and whale watching, as well as Hawaii's greatest gift to the world, the art of surfing.

Beaches

It's all too easy to forget that Maui's **beaches** can be deadly as well as beautiful, and you need to know exactly what you're doing before you enter the water. Unless you have local expertise, it's safest to swim at the official beach parks and most popular spots, especially those that are shielded by offshore reefs. Not all beaches have lifeguards and warning flags, and unattended beaches are not necessarily safe. Look for other bathers, but whatever your experience elsewhere, don't assume you'll be able to cope with the same conditions as the local kids. Always ask for advice and above all follow the cardinal rule – Never turn your back on the water.

The beaches that have the most accidents and drownings, such as Big Beach south of Mākena, tend to be those where waves of four feet or more break directly onto the shore. This varies according to the season, so beaches that are idyllic in summer can be storm-tossed death traps between October and April. If you get caught in a rip current or undertow and find yourself being dragged out to sea, stay calm and remember that the vast majority of such currents disappear within a hundred yards of the shore. Allow yourself to be carried out until the force weakens, and then swim first to one side and then back to the shore.

No one owns any stretch of beach in Hawaii. Every beach in the state – defined as the area below the vegetation line – is regarded as public property. That doesn't mean that you're entitled to stroll across any intervening land between the ocean and the nearest highway; always use the clearly signposted "public right of way" footpaths. Whatever impression the large oceanfront hotels may attempt to convey, they can't stop you from using the beaches out front; they can only restrict, but not refuse to supply, parking places for non-guests.

Surfing

Surf aficionados rate several Maui sites as equal to anything on Oahu's fabled North Shore, with Honolua Bay on the northern tip of West Maui, and Jaws off Ha'ikū in the east, as the greatest of all. You need to be a real expert to join the locals who surf there, however – beginners would do better to start out at Lahaina and Kā'anapali beaches. The peak season is between November and March.

Companies that offer surfing lessons in the Lahaina area include the Goofy Foot Surf School (☎808/244-9283, ⊛www.goofyfootsurfschool.com) and the Nancy Emerson School of Surfing (☎808/244-7873, ⊛www.surfclinics.com). South Maui instructors include Hawaiian Style Surf School (☎808/874-0110) and Maui Waveriders (☎808/875-4761, ⊛www.mauiwaveriders.com).

Windsurfing

Maui is renowned as the world's most sublime **windsurfing** destination. Legendary Ho'okipa Beach Park, just east of Pā'ia on the central isthmus, is a mecca for devotees and plays host to major championships throughout most of the year.

Strong winds are of greater importance to windsurfers than high surf, so summer is the peak season for the sport. Between December and February the winds tend to drop for days on end, but even then conditions are usually good enough somewhere on the island; Mā'alaea Bay on the south shore of the isthmus is the likeliest spot.

The best place to learn to windsurf is Kanahā Beach near Kahului, a few miles west of Ho'okipa. Expect to pay around $80 for a three-hour lesson (including equipment rental) with operators such as Action Sports Maui (☎ 808/871-5857, ⊛ www.actionsportsmaui.com), Alan Cadiz's HST Windsurfing School (☎ 808/871-5423 or 1-800/968-5423, ⊛ www.hstwindsurfing.com), Hawaiian Island Surf & Sport (☎808/871-4981 or 1-800/231-6958, ⊛ www.hawaiianisland.com), or Maui Ocean Activities (☎ 808/667-2001, ⊛ www.mauiwatersports.com).

Maui Windsurfari specializes in putting together all-inclusive packages for windsurfers (☎ 808/871-7766 or 1-800/736-6284, ⊛ www.windsurfari.com).

Diving

Maui and its immediate neighbors offer probably the best **scuba diving** in the Hawaiian islands. The most popular spots are in the vicinity of Molokini Crater, off South Maui. Learners and inexperienced divers start by exploring the sheltered, shallow "Inside Crater" area, and eventually progress to the "Back Wall," with its huge drop-offs. There's also good shore diving at Black Rock in Kā'anapali and in La Pérouse Bay, while the most spectacular dives of all lie off southern Lanai, within easy reach of a day's boat-trip from Maui.

A huge number of companies arrange diving excursions in the waters off Maui and Lanai, with the largest operator being Maui Dive Shop; full listings appear below. Prices generally start at around $80 for a one-tank trip, $100 for two tanks, with equipment rental costing an additional $25 or so. Almost all offer multi-day packages for beginners, leading to PADI certification; a typical price would be $220–250 for three days, and $300 for four. Bear in mind that many of the Molokini snorkel cruises listed on p.170 offer diving as well as snorkeling.

Be sure not to dive within 24 hours of flying or ascending to any significant altitude. The summit of Haleakalā is certainly out of bounds, while you should ask your dive operator for advice before even driving into the Upcountry.

Dive operators

Ed Robinson's Diving Adventures Kīhei ☎808/879-3584, ⊛www.mauiscuba.com
Extended Horizons Lahaina ☎1-888/348-3628, ⊛www.scubadivemaui.com
Lahaina Divers Lahaina ☎808/667-7496, ⊛www.lahainadivers.com
Maui Diamond Mā'alaea ☎1-866/879-9119, ⊛www.mauiscubatours.com

ESSENTIALS · Ocean sports

Maui Dive Shop Island-wide ☎808/879-1775, ⊛www.mauidiveshop.com
Maui Diving Lahaina ☎808/667-0633, ⊛www.mauidiving.com
Maui Sun Divers Kīhei ☎1-877/879-3337, ⊛http://mauisundivers.com
Mike Severn's Kīhei ☎808/879-6596, ⊛www.mikesevernsdiving.com
Pacific Dive Lahaina ☎808/667-5331, ⊛www.pacificdive.com
Trilogy Lahaina ☎1-888/225-6284, ⊛www.sailtrilogy.com

Parasailing

Parasailing, which is a bit like water-skiing, except you suddenly find yourself several hundred feet up in the air, has become very popular in the waters just off Kā'anapali and Lahaina in West Maui. To avoid disturbing humpback whales, however, it's only permitted between mid-May and mid-December. Expect to pay $40–50 for a fifteen-minute flight with operators such as Parasail Kā'anapali (☎808/669-6555), UFO Parasail (☎808/661-7836 or 1-800/359-4836, ⊛www.ufoparasailing.com), and Lahaina West Maui Parasail (☎808/661-4060).

Boat tours

Atlantis Submarines ☎808/667-2224 or 1-800/548-6262, ⊛www.atlantisadventures.com. One-hour underwater excursions off Lahaina ($80; look for discounts online).
Maui Princess ☎808/661-8397 or 1-877/500-6284, ⊛www.mauiprincess.com. Dinner ($79) and whale-watching ($19 and $31) cruises from Lahaina, plus one-day excursions to Molokai (from $80).
Pacific Whale Foundation ☎808/249-8811 or 1-800/942-5311, ⊛www.pacificwhale.org. This nonprofit organization offers 2–3hr whale-watching cruises from Lahaina or Mā'alaea (Nov–April; $20 and $30), plus snorkeling and dolphin-watching tours to Molokai (from $40) or Lanai ($75).
Reefdancer ☎808/667-2133. Sixty- or ninety-minute cruises ($33/$45) in a semi-submersible from Lahaina;

Molokini snorkel cruises

Maui's best-known snorkeling and diving spot is the tiny crescent of **Molokini**, three miles off Mākena. Created by a volcanic eruption 230,000 years ago, it consists of half of a once-circular crater wall, poking 162ft above the waves. There's no beach or landfall of any kind, but you see a lot of fish, including deep-water species.

Countless cruises leave early each morning from Mā'alaea Harbor. It's also possible to take a significantly longer and more expensive cruise from Lahaina, while the very shortest crossing departs from Mākena's *Maui Prince* hotel (see p.157).

All the companies listed below operate out of Mā'alaea. Snorkelers can pay anything from $50 to $110 for a five- to six-hour morning trip, depending on the size and comfort of the boat and the refreshments offered, and from $35 for a shorter afternoon jaunt; scuba divers pay around $40 extra. Between November and April, many companies stop running Molokini trips and concentrate on lucrative whale-watching cruises instead.

Boat	Phone	⊛www.	Passengers
Frogman II	☎808/661-3333	bossfrog.com	52
Hokua	☎808/249-2583	alohabluecharters.com	20
Lahaina Princess	☎877/500-6284	mauiprincess.com	100
Lani Kai	☎808/244-1979	mauisnorkeling.com	70
Leilani	☎808/242-0935	prideofmaui.com	49
Ocean Odyssey	☎808/249-8811	pacificwhale.org	149
Ocean Spirit	☎808/249-8811	pacificwhale.org	142
Paragon II	☎808/244-2087	sailmaui.com	35
Pride of Maui	☎808/242-0955	prideofmaui.com	149
Prince Kuhio	☎808/242-8777	mvprince.com	149
Quicksilver	☎808/661-3333	bossfrog.com	142

Equipment rental

Auntie Snorkel 2439 S Kīhei Rd, Kīhei ☏808/879-6263 or 1-877/256-4248, ✆www.auntiesnorkel.com. Choose from snorkels and kayaks.

Boss Frog's Dive Shop 1215 S Kīhei Rd, Kīhei ☏808/891-0077; 2395 S Kīhei Rd, Kīhei ☏808/875-4477; 150 Lahainaluna Rd, Lahaina ☏808/661-3333; 3636 Lower Honoapi'ilani Rd, Kā'anapali ☏808/665-1200; 4310 Lower Honoapi'ilani Rd, Kahana ☏808/669-6700; and Nāpili Plaza, Nāpili ☏808/669-4949; ✆www .bossfrog.com. Activity center that also rents out scuba, snorkeling and surf gear.

Maui Dive Shop 1455 S Kīhei Rd, Kīhei ☏808/879-3388; Honokōwai Marketplace, 3350 Lower Honoapi'ilani Rd ☏808/661-6166; and five other Maui locations; ✆www.mauidiveshop.com.

Dive specialists who rent scuba and snorkeling equipment.

Snorkel Bob's 1279 S Kīhei Rd, Kīhei ☏808/875-6188; 2411 S Kīhei Rd, Kīhei ☏808/879-7449; 1217 Front St, Lahaina ☏808/661-4421; and *Nāpili Village Hotel*, 5425 Lower Honoapi'ilani Rd, Nāpili ☏808/669-9603; ✆www .snorkelbob.com. Their snorkel gear can be returned on any island.

South Pacific Kayaks Rainbow Mall, 2439 S Kīhei Rd ☏808/875-4848, ✆www.southpacifickayaks.com. Choose from kayaks, surfboards, snorkels, boogie boards, beach chairs, and the like.

West Maui Cycles 1087 Limahana Place, Lahaina ☏808/661-9005, ✆www .westmauicycles.com. Besides mountain bikes, you'll find snorkels, boogie boards, and surfboards.

passengers view the reef from an underwater cabin.

Trilogy Ocean Sports ☏808/661-4743 or 1-888/225-6284, ✆www.sailtrilogy.com. Day-long sailing trips from Lahaina to Lanai, including snorkeling, beach barbecue, and Lanai van tour ($179). They also offer diving and snorkeling at Molokini and off Lanai.

Kayak tours

Kelii's Kayak Tours ☏1-888/874-7652, ✆www.keliiskayak.com. Two-hour kayak tours ($49) from Lahaina, plus several more options in West, North, and South Maui, culminating in a $129 kayaking expedition to Molokini.

South Pacific Kayaks Rainbow Mall, 2439 S Kīhei Rd ☏808/875-4848 or 1-800/776-2326, ✆www.southpacifickayaks.com. An extensive range of kayaking tours, from 2hr 15min whale-watching trips ($65; in season only) via 3hr guided excursions at Mākena or Lahaina, up to extended tours in South or West Maui for up to $99.

Land activities

Downhill biking

For over twenty years, one of Maui's most unusual and popular tourist activities has been to take a minivan to the top of Haleakalā – especially at dawn – and then climb onto a **bike** and ride, or rather coast, back down the mountain. It's possible to make it all the way down to the ocean at Pā'ia, a 39-mile ride, without pedaling. The descent can be great fun, although some tend to

find it a bit pointless, as to comply with park-service regulations most operators make their groups ride together, at the pace of the slowest member. Other drawbacks include the chilly temperatures on the mountain (though all the companies supply protective gear) and the *very* early starts for the sunrise tours; hotel pick-ups can be as early as 2am – hardly conducive to a happy family atmosphere.

The usual activities desks, such as Tom Barefoot's (see box below), offer discount rates on biking trips: typical rates range from around $70 for a daytime ride up to $120 to go at sunrise. Unguided trips, or shorter routes, cost about $20 less. All riders must have at least some biking experience, and be aged 12 or over.

Bike tours from the crater

Only the four operators below are currently permitted to start their trips from the crater itself. All offer fully guided group trips only, and include hotel pick-ups from West or South Maui.

Cruiser Phil's ☎808/893-2332 or 1-877/764-2453, ✆www.cruiserphil.com. Sunrise and daytime tours, all the way to Pā'ia.

Maui Downhill ☎808/871-2155 or 1-800/535-2453, ✆www.mauidownhill.com. Long tours, including hotel pick-up and usually lunch as well, to Pā'ia or Kula.

Maui Mountain Cruisers ☎808/871-6014 or 1-800/232-6284, ✆www.mauimountaincruisers.com. Sunrise or morning downhill rides to Pā'ia.

Mountain Riders Bike Tours ☎808/242-9739 or 1-800/706-7700, ✆www.mountainriders.com. Sunrise and morning tours down Haleakalā, with or without guides, and ending at Pā'ia, Kula, or Tedeschi Winery.

Bike tours from the base of Haleakalā

Though it's not always clear from their brochures, the following companies offer trips on which you only see the summit itself as part of a van tour, and you actually start cycling from the edge of the park, eleven miles below. This makes for a warmer, cheaper, and potentially shorter ride, and as you don't necessarily have to be guided or accompanied, can also mean that you get to do some genuine cycling around the Upcountry.

Aloha Bike Tours ☎808/249-0911 or 1-800/749-1564, ✆www.mauibike.com. Small-group tours, starting below the summit and ending at Tedeschi Winery rather than the sea.

Haleakalā Bike Co. ☎808/575-9575 or 1-888/922-2453, ✆www.bikemaui.com. Unguided tours; they provide the bikes and a van tour to the top, then drop you at the park entrance, from where you descend at your own pace.

Upcountry Cycles ☎808/573-2888 or 1-800/373-1678, ✆www.bikemauihawaii.com. Unguided rides, at sunrise or in the morning, and also bike rentals.

Horse riding

Ironwood Ranch ☎808/669-4991 or 1-877/699-4529, ✆www.ironwoodranch.com. Riding excursions up to the forest above Kapalua, at $80 for 1hr 30min, $110 for 2hr, or $150 for the advanced "Ironwood Odyssey."

Lahaina Stables ☎808/667-2222, ✆www.mauihorse.com. Horseback adventures on the slopes of the West Maui mountains above Lahaina; two-hour morning rides for $110 or sunset rides for $120, 3hr 30min morning rides for $135.

Mākena Stables ☎808/879-0244, ✆www.makenastables.com. Two- to three–hour morning or evening rides along the coastline from 'Āhihi Bay, south of Big Beach, to La Pérouse, or 5hr 30min trips up to Ulupalakua Ranch; $120–195. No credit cards. Mon–Sat.

Maui Horseback Tours ☎808/248-7799, ✆www.mauistables.com. Three-hour riding tours with an emphasis on Hawaiian history and spirituality, in the remote but beautiful Kīpahulu district, west of 'Ohe'o Gulch in East Maui. Departs 9.30am and 1pm daily, $150.

Mendes Ranch ☎808/871-5222, ✆www.mendesranch.com. Half-day tours of this cattle ranch in East Maui's Waihe'e Valley, with barbecue lunch; $130 per person or $219 with a 30min helicopter flight. Shorter 2hr tours cost $89. Mon–Sat.

Discount activities

Activities operators in all the tourist areas, especially along Front Street in Lahaina, offer **cut-price deals** well below the advertised rates. Tom Barefoot's Cashback Tours – at 834 Front St, Lahaina (☎808/661-8889 or 1-888/222-3601, ✆www.tombarefoot.com) – is one of the few that don't also try to sell time-shares, and its website details every imaginable island activity, along with the latest prices.

Pony Express Tours ☎808/667-2200, @www.ponyexpresstours.com. One-hour ($65), 2hr ($95), and 2hr 30min (with picnic; $115) tours of Haleakalā Ranch, Maui's largest cattle ranch (Mon–Fri). 5hr 30min descent to Ka Moa O Pele junction in Haleakalā Crater ($169) or 8hr trip to Kapalaoa Cabin ($195), both with picnic lunch (Mon–Sat).

Hang-gliding

Hang Gliding Maui is a one-man operation that provides powered **hang-gliding** lessons from Hāna airport in East Maui, at $115 for 30min, $190 for 1hr (☎ 808/572-6557, @ www.hanggliding maui.com). The most popular spot for experienced practitioners to do some traditional hang-gliding is Polipoli State Park in the Upcountry (see p.107).

ATV tours

'Ulupalakua Ranch in Upcountry Maui (see p.109) is the base for Maui ATV Tours, which offers off-road tours in **all-terrain vehicles**, either as part of a convoy of individual buggies, or as a group in a rugged truck. Tours explore backcountry areas both down by the ocean and up in the Upcountry (daily; 4-hour tour starting at 8am, $130 with lunch; 2-hour tour starting at 2pm, $94; over-16s only; ☎ 808/878-2889; @ www.mauiatvtours .com).

Skyline

One of Maui's most enjoyable outdoor attractions is based in the Upcountry, 2.5 miles up Haleakalā Crater Road from the point where it leaves Hwy-377. With Skyline Eco Adventures, you hike into the woodlands of Haleakalā Ranch, where you're harnessed up to ride a succession of lengthy "ziplines" across remote gullies. It's a truly breathtaking experience, though you'll have to have a head for heights to be prepared to take the initial death-defying leap ($79; ☎ 808/878-8475, @www.skylinehawaii.com).

Golf

The spectacular oceanfront **golf courses** at Maui's major resorts, designed to tournament specifications but open to all, have the highest reputations, but they also have the highest greens fees – all are well over $100, and the reductions for hotel guests are not all that significant. Rates at municipal courses, by contrast, can start as low as $50, while typical public courses charge upwards of $50 per round, with reduced rates early in the morning and last thing at night. All courses charge lower rates for Hawaii residents, and some charge extra premiums for foreign nationals. TeeTimes Hawaii (☎1-888/675-GOLF or 808/922-0431, @ www.teetimeshawaii.com) specializes in finding discounted and short-notice golfing opportunities.

You can find details of Maui's golf courses online at @ www.guidetogolf .net. The listings are produced by the PGA (@ www.pgatour.com), whose free brochure *The PGA Tour Guide to Golf* is widely available, for example at airport information racks, throughout the islands.

Maui golf courses

	Area	Holes	Kind	Fee	Phone
Dunes at Maui Lani	Kahului	18	Public	$96	☎808/873-0422
Elleair Golf Course	Kīhei	18	Public	$90	☎808/874-0777
Kā'anapali Golf Course					
North Course	Kā'anapali	18	Resort	$150	☎808/661-3691
South Course	Kā'anapali	18	Resort	$142	☎808/661-3691
Kapalua Golf Club					
Bay Course	Kapalua	18	Resort	$180	☎808/669-8820
Plantation Course	Kapalua	18	Resort	$220	☎808/669-8877
Village Course	Kapalua	18	Resort	$160	☎808/669-8835
Maui Country Club	Pā'ia	9	Private	$75	☎808/877-7893
Pukalani Country Club	Upcountry	18	Public	$55	☎808/572-1314
Sandalwood Golf Course	Waikapū	18	Public	$80	☎808/242-7090
Wai'ehu Municipal Golf Course	Wailuku	18	Municipal	$30	☎808/243-7400
Wailea Golf Club					
Blue Course	Wailea	18	Resort	$145	☎808/875-7450
Emerald Course	Wailea	18	Resort	$160	☎808/875-7450
Gold Course	Wailea	18	Resort	$160	☎808/875-7450

Entertainment

Although island residents jokingly refer to the hour of 10pm as "Maui midnight," by Hawaiian standards Maui offers visitors a reasonably lively **nightlife**.

As ever, most of the activity is confined to the tourist enclaves, and the resort hotels in particular, but if you enjoy wandering the streets from bar to bar the oceanfront at **Lahaina** will be right up your street. The south coast, from **Kīhei** on down, is too spread out to have the same intensity, but it's always party time somewhere along the strip – and especially around the downmarket but fun Kīhei Kalama Village mall.

Lovers of traditional Hawaiian music should head to the *Ritz-Carlton* in Kapalua, which stages an excellent series of weekly **slack key guitar** concerts, as described on p.71. More contemporary Hawaiian sounds can be heard at *Hapa's Brew Haus* in Kīhei, while the *Tsunami* at the *Grand Wailea* resort in Wailea is renowned as Maui's glitziest nightclub.

Away from the resorts, the local community of rock exiles and ex-Californians makes *Casanova's* in upcountry **Makawao** an amazingly happening venue for such a tiny town. There's also the Maui Arts and Cultural Center by the harbor in **Kahului**, which attracts big-name touring bands.

Festivals and events

Note that the exact dates of surfing contests, and in some cases the venues as well, depend on wave conditions.

January
Maui Pro Surf Meet; surfing competition, Honolua Bay and Ho'okipa Beach

3rd week in January
Hula Bowl Football All-Star Classic; college football tournament, War Memorial Stadium, Wailuku

Early February
Whale Fest Week; whale-related events, Lahaina and Kā'anapali

Late February
Maui Classical Music Festival, Maui Arts & Cultural Center

March
Run to the Sun; foot race, Pā'ia to Haleakalā

March/April
East Maui Taro Festival, Hāna (@www.tarofestival.org)

Late April
David Malo Day, Lahainaluna High School, Lahaina
Maui County Agricultural Trade Show, Ulupalakua Ranch

Late May
Bankoh Ho'omana'o Challenge; outrigger canoe race, Kā'anapali to Waikīkī
In Celebration of Canoes, Lahaina

Mid-June
Maui Film Festival, Wailea

June
Kiho'alu; slack key guitar festival, Maui Arts & Cultural Center

July 4
Makawao Rodeo, Makawao

Early July
Quicksilver Cup; windsurfing competition, Kanahā Beach

Early August
Hawaii State Championships; windsurfing competition, Kanahā Beach

Mid-September
A Taste of Lahaina; food festival, Lahaina

Late September
Maui Marathon, Kahului to Kā'anapali

Early October
Maui County Fair, Wailuku

Mid-October
Aloha Festival

October 31
Halloween Mardi Gras of the Pacific, Lahaina

Late October/early November
Aloha Classic World Wavesailing Championships; windsurfing competition, Ho'okipa

Public holidays

Jan 1 New Year's Day
Third Mon in Jan Martin Luther King Day
Third Mon in Feb Presidents' Day
March 26 Prince Kuhio Day
Easter Monday
May 1 Lei Day
Last Mon in May Memorial Day
June 11 Kamehameha Day

July 4 Independence Day
Third Fri in Aug Admission Day
First Mon in Sept Labor Day
Second Mon in Oct Columbus Day
Nov 11 Veterans Day
Last Thurs in Nov Thanksgiving Day
Dec 25 Christmas Day

Shopping

If you have come to Hawaii specifically to **shop**, the stores of Maui may not meet your needs. The state's premier malls are concentrated in Honolulu on Oahu, and unless you go there as well, you may fly home with fewer gifts and souvenirs than you expected. The prints, posters, and T-shirts on sale in Lahaina and the major tourist areas are OK if you think that whales are interplanetary voyagers from another dimension, or that a gecko on a surfboard is real neat, but stores and galleries selling high-quality indigenous arts and crafts are few and far between. Pā'ia and Makawao are the most likely towns to find interesting or unusual gifts.

Maui's largest malls are the Ka'ahumanu Mall and the Maui Marketplace in Kahului, though the most upmarket individual stores are in the Shops at Wailea mall, or in individual resort hotels.

Hawaiian crafts

Some of the most attractive products of Hawaii are just too ephemeral to take home. That goes for the orchids and tropical flowers on sale everywhere, and unfortunately it's also true of *leis*.

Leis (pronounced *lays*) are flamboyant decorative garlands, usually consisting of flowers such as the fragrant *melia* (the plumeria or frangipani) or the Big Island's own bright-red *lehua* blossom (from the *'ō'hia* tree), but sometimes also made from feathers, shells, seeds, or nuts. Both men and women wear them, above all on celebrations or gala occasions. The days are gone when every arriving tourist was festooned with a *lei*, but you'll probably be way-*leied* at a *lū'au* or some such occasion, while on Lei Day (May 1) everyone's at it.

Colorful Hawaiian clothing, such as **aloha shirts** and the cover-all "Mother-Hubbard"-style *mu'umu'u* dress, is on sale everywhere, though classic designs are surprisingly rare and you tend to see the same stylized prints over and over again. Sig Zane's store in Wailuku (see p.81) is the best source of out-of-the-ordinary *aloha* wear.

Otherwise, the main local crafts are **lau hala** weaving, in which mats, hats, baskets, and the like are created by plaiting the large leaves (*lau*) of the spindly-legged pandanus (*hala*) tree, and **wood turning**, with fine bowls made from native dark woods such as *koa*.

Directory

Electricity Hawaii's electricity supply, like that on the US mainland, uses 100 volts AC. Plugs are standard American two-pins.
Gay and lesbian life Much the greatest concentration of gay activism in Hawaii is in Honolulu, though the state as a whole is liberal on gay issues. It's one of 25 states to allow consensual "sodomy," with no criminal laws against private sex acts and a guarantee of privacy in the constitution. Maui hotels geared towards gay travelers include the *Wailana Inn* and the *Sunseeker Resort*, close neighbors in Kīhei (see p.157). Pacific Ocean

Holidays (PO Box 88245, Honolulu HI 96830-8245 ☎808/923-2400 or 1-800/735-6600, ◍www.gayhawaii.com) organizes all-inclusive package vacations in Hawaii for gay and lesbian travelers, while their website is an invaluable source of listings.
Hospitals Maui hospitals can be contacted on the following numbers: Wailuku ☎808/244-9056; Kula ☎808/878-1221; Hāna ☎808/248-8294. In emergencies call ☎911.
Inoculations No inoculations or vaccinations are required by law in order to enter

Hawaii, though some authorities suggest a polio vaccination.

Internet access Internet access is widely available. Most public libraries offer it for free; hostels tend to have a computer or two where guests can check email; and both copier outlets and Internet cafés allow customers to go online.

Mail Mail service between Maui and the rest of the world is extremely slow, as all mail is routed via Honolulu. Allow a week for your letter to reach destinations in the US and as much as two weeks or more for the rest of the world.

There are post offices In Lahaina at 132 Papalaua St, in the Lahaina Shopping Center (Mon–Fri 8.15am–4.15pm); in Kahului at 138 S Pu'unēnē Ave (Mon–Fri 8.30am–5pm, Sat 9am–noon); in Wailuku at 250 Imi Kala St (Mon–Fri 8am–4.30pm, Sat 9am–noon); and in Hāna at the Hāna Ranch Center (Mon–Fri 8am–4.30pm; Hāna HI 96713).

Public toilets Some public toilets are labeled in Hawaiian: *Kanes* means Men, *Wahines* means Women.

Quarantine Very stringent restrictions apply to the importation of all plants and animals into Hawaii. Cats and dogs must stay in quarantine for 120 days; if you were hoping to bring an alligator or a hamster into the state, forget it. For full regulations call ☏808/871-5656.

Senior travelers US residents aged 50 or over can join the American Association of Retired Persons, 601 E St NW, Washington, DC 20049 (☏1-800/424-3410; ⊛www .aarp.org), for discounts on accommodation and vehicle rental.

Telephones The telephone area code for the entire state of Hawaii is ☏808. Calls within Maui count as local; you don't need to dial the area code and it costs a flat-rate 50¢ on pay phones. The cheapest long-distance rates apply between 11pm and 8am from Monday to Thursday and between 5pm Friday and 8am Monday; an intermediate rate applies between 5pm and 11pm from Monday to Thursday.

Hotels impose huge surcharges, so it's best to use a phone card for long-distance calls. In preference to the ones issued by the major phone companies, you'll find it simpler and cheaper to choose from the various pre-paid cards sold in almost all supermarkets and general stores.

Time Unlike most of the United States, Hawaii does not observe Daylight Saving Time. Therefore, from 2am on the last Sunday in April until 2am on the last Sunday in October, the time difference between Hawaii and the US West Coast is three hours, not the usual two; and the islands are six hours later than the East Coast, not five. Hawaiian time is from ten to eleven hours behind the UK.

Tipping Wait staff in restaurants expect tips of fifteen percent, in bars a little less. Hotel porters and bellhops should receive around $2 per piece of luggage and housekeeping staff $2 per night.

Travelers with disabilities The State of Hawaii Disability and Communication Access Board produces a wide range of reports on facilities for disabled travelers on each of the islands, which you can download from their website (☏808/586-8121, ⊛www.state.hi.us/health/dcab/). In addition, Access–Able (⊛www.access–able.com) carries detailed reports on the accessibility of hotels and other facilities throughout Hawaii.

Weddings To get married in Hawaii, you must have a valid state licence, which costs $50 from the Department of Health, Marriage License Office, 1250 Punchbowl St, Honolulu HI 96813 (☏808/586-4545, ⊛www.hawaii.gov/doh), and is valid for thirty days. To find an agent on Maui who can issue a licence, call ☏808/984-8210. You also need proof of rubella immunizations or screening, which can be arranged through the Department of Health. Most resorts offer their own marriage planners, or you can pick up a full list of companies that specialize in arranging weddings by visiting the Maui Wedding Association online (⊛www.mauiweddingassociation.com).

Advertiser

ROUGH GUIDES TRAVEL...

Rough Guides are available from good bookstores worldwide. New titles are
published every month. Check www.roughguides.com for the latest news

...MUSIC & REFERENCE

Also! More than 120 Rough Guide music CDs are available from all good book and record stores. Listen in at www.worldmusic.net

small print & **Index**

A Rough Guide to Rough Guides

Las Vegas DIRECTIONS is published by Rough Guides. The first *Rough Guide to Greece*, published in 1982, was a student scheme that became a publishing phenomenon. The immediate success of the book – with numerous reprints and a Thomas Cook prize short-listing – spawned a series that rapidly covered dozens of destinations. Rough Guides had a ready market among low-budget backpackers, but soon also acquired a much broader and older readership that relished Rough Guides' wit and inquisitiveness as much as their enthusiastic, critical approach. Everyone wants value for money, but not at any price. Rough Guides soon began supplementing the "rougher" information about hostels and low-budget listings with the kind of detail on restaurants and quality hotels that independent-minded visitors on any budget might expect, whether on business in New York or trekking in Thailand. These days the guides offer recommendations from shoestring to luxury and cover a large number of destinations around the globe, including almost every country in the Americas and Europe, more than half of Africa and most of Asia and Australasia. Rough Guides now publish:

- Travel guides to more than 200 worldwide destinations
- Dictionary phrasebooks to 22 major languages
- Maps printed on rip-proof and waterproof Polyart™ paper
- Music guides running the gamut from Opera to Elvis
- Reference books on topics as diverse as the Weather and Shakespeare
- World Music CDs in association with World Music Network

Visit www.roughguides.com to see our latest publications.

Publishing information

This 1st edition published October 2005 by **Rough Guides Ltd**, 80 Strand, London WC2R 0RL. 345 Hudson St, 4th Floor, New York, NY 10014, USA. 14 Local Shopping Centre, Panchsheel Park, New Delhi 110017, India.

Distributed by the Penguin Group
Penguin Books Ltd, 80 Strand, London WC2R 0RL
Penguin Group (USA), 375 Hudson Street, NY 10014, USA
Penguin Group (Australia), 250 Camberwell Road, Camberwell, Victoria 3124, Australia
Penguin Group (Canada), 10 Alcorn Avenue, Toronto, ON M4V 1E4, Canada
Penguin Group (New Zealand), Cnr Rosedale and Airborne Roads, Albany, Auckland, New Zealand
Typeset in Bembo and Helvetica to an original design by Henry Iles.
Printed and bound in China

© Greg Ward, October 2005

No part of this book may be reproduced in any form without permission from the publisher except for the quotation of brief passages in reviews.
192pp includes index

A catalogue record for this book is available from the British Library

ISBN-13: 978-1-84353-512-6
ISBN-10: 1-84353-512-2

The publishers and author have done their best to ensure the accuracy and currency of all the information in **Maui DIRECTIONS**, however, they can accept no responsibility for any loss, injury, or inconvenience sustained by any traveler as a result of information or advice contained in the guide.

1   3   5   7   9   8   6   4   2

Help us update

We've gone to a lot of effort to ensure that the first edition of **Maui DIRECTIONS** is accurate and up-to-date. However, things change – places get "discovered," opening hours are notoriously fickle, restaurants and rooms raise prices or lower standards. If you feel we've got it wrong or left something out, we'd like to know, and if you can remember the address, the price, the phone number, so much the better.
We'll credit all contributions, and send a copy of the next edition (or any other DIRECTIONS guide or Rough Guide if you prefer) for the best letters. Everyone who writes to us and isn't already a subscriber will receive a copy of our full-color thrice-yearly newsletter. Please mark letters: **"Maui DIRECTIONS Update"** and send to: Rough Guides, 80 Strand, London WC2R 0RL, or Rough Guides, 4th Floor, 345 Hudson St, New York, NY 10014. Or send an email to mail@roughguides.com
Have your questions answered and tell others about your trip at www.roughguides.atinfopop.com

Rough Guide credits

Text editor: Steven Horak
Layout: Amit Verma
Photography: James McConnachie and Greg Ward
Cartography: Jai Prakash Mishra

Picture editor: Jj Luck
Proofreader: Diane Margolis
Production: Katherine Owers
Design: Henry Iles
Cover design: Chloë Roberts

SMALL PRINT

The author

Greg Ward has written and taken photos for all four editions of the Rough Guide to Hawaii, and two previous Rough Guides to Maui, and also guides to the Big Island and Oahu, as well as Rough Guides to Las Vegas, Southwest USA, The Grand Canyon, Blues CDs, the History of the USA, and Brittany and Normandy. He has also co-written guides to the USA and Online Travel; edited the USA, India and Elvis guides among others; and worked for several other guide-book publishers.

Acknowledgments

Thanks and love as ever to Samantha Cook at home, in the year of our marriage; to Steven Horak for his scrupulous, efficient, and friendly editing; to James McConnachie for his excellent photos and extra help; Jj Luck for her picture research; Jai Prakash Mishra and Katie Lloyd-Jones for the maps; and to Amit Verma for his typesetting. It wouldn't be possible to write such a detailed guide without the very great help of many people in Maui; among those I'd like to thank especially are Nicole LaBerge; Lori Michimoto; Scott Innes; Candy Aluli; Donica; Cherie; Rebecca Huska; Kalani Nakoa; Michael Tuttle; and Danny Boren.

James McConnachie would also like to thank Nane Aluli, Wendy Bagwill, Brenda Boroso, Judy Edwards, Paul Konwiser, Roxanne Murayama, Allan Muhlach, Sherry, Ashley Stepanek, and Julie Yoneyama.

Photo credits

Index

Maps are marked in color

INDEX